THE BATTLE FOR LIMERICK CITY

MILITARY HISTORY
OF THE IRISH CIVIL WAR

THE BATTLE FOR LIMERICK CITY

Pádraig Óg Ó Ruairc

SERIES EDITOR: GABRIEL DOHERTY

MERCIER PRESS
IRISH PUBLISHER – IRISH STORY

MERCIER PRESS

Cork

www.mercierpress.ie

Trade enquiries to CMD BookSource,

55a Spruce Avenue, Stillorgan Industrial Park,

Blackrock, County Dublin

© Pádraig Óg Ó Ruairc, 2010

© Foreword: Gabriel Doherty, 2010

ISBN: 978 1 85635 675 6

10 9 8 7 6 5 4 3 2 1

A CIP record for this title is available from the British Library

Printed and bound in the EU.

For Deirdre & Liam.
Wishing you not civil strife,
But many happy years together.

CONTENTS

War with the foreigner brings to the fore all that is best and noblest in a nation. Civil War all that is mean and base.

Frank Aiken in a letter to the Provisional Free State
Government, 3 August 1922[1]

Lloyd George was really right in what he did, if we had gone on we could probably have squashed the rebellion as a temporary measure, but it would have broken out again like an ulcer the moment we removed the troops. I think the rebels would probably have refused battles, and hidden away their arms, etc., until we had gone. The only way therefore was to give them some form of self government and let them squash the rebellion themselves; they were the only people who could really stamp it out, and they are still trying to do so and as far as one can tell they seem to be having a fair amount of success. I am not, however, in close touch with the situation over there, but it seems to me they had more success than we had.

Letter from Field Marshal Bernard Law Montgomery to
Major Percival, 14 October 1923[2]

ACKNOWLEDGEMENTS

I wish to thank the following:

My parents, Pat and Monica. My siblings Deirdre and Kevin. Eoin Purcell whose concept this book was. Tom Toomey, Thomas Mac Con Mara, Jim Corbett, Danny McCarthy, Martin 'Bob' O'Dwyer, Donal O'Flynn, Liz Gillis, Cormac Ó Comhraí, Des Long, William Butler, Miceál O'Hurley-Pitts, Seán O'Hehir, Jeremiah Hurley, Terry O'Reilly, Declan Barron, Seán Ó Murchada, Pat Gunn, Dr Ruan O'Donnell, Dr John O'Callaghan and all the other historians I know who are so generous with their time, advice and information. John White, Chris Coe, Cyril Wall, Aidan Larkin, Mick Houlihan, Billy McGlynn, Andrew Clancy, Johnny White, Connor Farrell, Gavin O'Connell, Dara Macken, Maurice Quinlivan, Liam Hogan, Jim Forde, Séamus Welsh, Sean Curtin, Martin and Norma Naughton, Seán Gannon, 'The Rubberbandits', the staff of Charles Fort, but especially Karen, Brendan, Claire and Evelyn, the two Marys in Dungarvan, Brian Hodkinson and the staff of the Limerick Civic Museum; Mike Maguire at the Local Studies department, Limerick City Library; the staff of the Irish Military Archives;

the National Library of Ireland; the staff of the National Archives; the staff of Kilmainham Jail Museum; Peter at the Clare Local Studies Centre; all the staff of the Clare Library; the Khaki and Green War of Independence Re-enactors, especially Éamonn Dunne and Ray Murphy; Seán O'Mahony and the 1916–1921 Club; Francis E. Maguire for giving me permission to use extracts from John Pinkman's diaries; Mary, Patrick and Wendy and all the staff of Mercier Press.

FOREWORD

It is a truism that the defining feature of the Irish Civil War was that it was, indeed, a *war*. That is, it is undeniable that the salient characteristic of life in Ireland between the attack on the Four Courts on 28 June 1922 and the 'dump arms' order issued to the IRA by its chief-of-staff, Frank Aiken, on 24 May 1923, was the existence of a state of (to quote but one, brief dictionary definition) 'armed hostile conflict', involving the use of destructive lethal force by belligerent parties. That it is necessary to draw attention to this apparently self-evident fact will be surprising to many, but some of the (very fine) scholarship on the subject of these seminal eleven months that has been produced over the last decade – focused as such writings have been on political developments or socio-psychological dimensions to the Treaty split – have, by accident or design, tended to elide this base-line fact. This omission does not, of course, make such works 'wrong'; at worst it makes them incomplete – and bearing in mind Clausewitz's mandatory dictum that war is simply the extension of politics by other means, a strong case might be made that the specifically martial aspects of the conflict are, indeed, of secondary importance. The lacuna, however, remains striking, and all the more so when one considers the numerous, and extremely welcome, publications on military aspects of the War of Independence that have appeared in the last two to three years (many of which, I am delighted to note, can be attributed to the industry and acumen of Mercier Press).

This omission is, of course, nothing new; on the contrary, it is entirely consistent with what went before – or, more accurately, what didn't. One of the most insidious legacies of the Civil War was the want for decades of a dispassionate analysis of the causes, course, and consequences of its military aspects; not surprisingly, partisan accounts were, by way of contrast, plentiful and even more insidious. The reasons for this absence were numerous and entirely understandable. They include the determination of the Cumann na nGaedheal government to deny its enemies in the IRA the retrospective comfort of implied belligerent status; the bitterness of republicans at the memory of what was, after all, a crushing defeat; public aversion at the excesses perpetrated by both sides; and the general realisation that the cherished (if tenuous) unity of the 'four glorious years' had been lost forever, to the extent that it had meaningfully existed at all. Ground-breaking general studies by Calton Younger and Michael Hopkinson subsequently facilitated an atmosphere more conducive to evidence-based discussion, although both were handicapped (as, indeed, were researchers in many other fields of historical enquiry) by the failure of the state for many decades to open its archives to independent inspection. The eruption of violence in Northern Ireland in the late 1960s was another factor that helped to extend the shelf-life of Ireland's Great Silence.

This new series, specifically examining the military aspects of the Civil War, is intended to address this obvious gap in modern Irish historiography. Covering all the principal local theatres, with an obvious focus on the battle for Munster where the majority of the fighting took place, each volume will discuss the fighting strength and tactics of the opposing forces, and focus as much on the human dimensions to the combat (in terms of death, injuries and personal experiences) as on the political and strategic significance of each engagement. Taken collectively they will offer innovative insights into a topic that has been hidden in plain view for too long.

In your hands you hold the first volume to appear in the series. It focuses on the fight for Limerick, a city not unused to military engagements or unfamiliar with disputed treaties, and a veritable cockpit of republican enmities in the spring of 1922. It is a story by turns suspenseful, awful and heart-rending, and is adroitly narrated by the author, Pádraig Óg Ó Ruairc. It is a fine point of departure for a series that will, I believe, capture the wide audience it merits.

Gabriel Doherty
Department of History
University College Cork

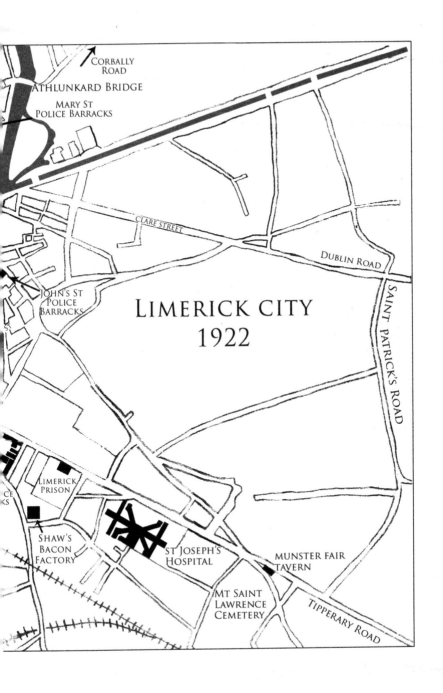

CORBALLY ROAD

ATHLUNKARD BRIDGE

MARY ST POLICE BARRACKS

CLARE STREET

DUBLIN ROAD

JOHN'S ST POLICE BARRACKS

LIMERICK CITY 1922

SAINT PATRICK'S ROAD

LIMERICK PRISON

SHAW'S BACON FACTORY

ST JOSEPH'S HOSPITAL

MUNSTER FAIR TAVERN

MT SAINT LAWRENCE CEMETERY

TIPPERARY ROAD

CHAPTER 1

THE BRITISH WITHDRAWAL

The remaining light was fading on a dreary February evening in Limerick city as a British army sentry from the Royal Welch Fusiliers stood high above the River Shannon on the walls of King John's Castle. He watched with disinterest as the carefree townspeople sauntered across Thomond bridge below him in twos and threes. There was no haste, no clatter of hobnailed boots on cobblestones; the passers-by seemed at ease. Soft footsteps tapping on stone in the twilight. Young lovers wandered out on their evening walk, arm in arm, passing the city's workers who shared cigarettes on their way home, nosily debating the merits of each pub in an effort to decide which one they should call to until some 'wag' finished the argument by loudly declaring they should have a drink in each one. On the north bank of the

Shannon smart comments and biting insults were hurled at the passers-by from a group of corner boys sitting at the foot of the Treaty Stone. Occasionally these reached the soldier's ears from across the river and he gave a wry smile when he managed to hear enough of the joke. For once he enjoyed the fact that the insults of the townspeople were not reserved for himself and his comrades.

The soldier hooked the canvas sling of his Lee Enfield rifle with the thumb of his right hand, readjusting the weapon to a more comfortable position on his shoulder. Then he unbuttoned the left breast pocket of his uniform tunic and withdrew a cigarette. He pressed a match against the Castle's ancient stones, but he paused for a moment when a thought suddenly struck him. Years of experience in the trenches of the First World War and on patrol in Ireland had taught him that the flare of a match was enough to draw the attention of an enemy sniper. Still motionless he considered the prospect. There was peace in Ireland now, but a very uneasy peace. Only the week before the IRA had shot dead a Scottish Black and Tan named McEdward in Garryowen, and just two months before that the IRA had assassinated an RIC sergeant in Kilmallock named Enright. Republican breaches of the ceasefire were becoming more and more common.

Finally, having weighed up the odds, he decided that it was unlikely there were any IRA gunmen lurking in the shadows, he struck the match, raised it to the cigarette and braced his back against the wall to enjoy his smoke. Soon he would be back home on leave or in a quieter posting free from such cares.

Seven hundred years before when the British colonisation of Ireland began, Norman crossbow men would have stood at the same place on the Castle walls on sentry duty. But now, after centuries of struggle, rebellion and war the 2nd Battalion of the Royal Welch Fusiliers would be the last British troops to occupy the Castle. For over two years, from 1919 to 1921, the Irish Republican Army had waged a guerrilla campaign against the might of the British Empire, the largest empire the world had ever seen. The republicans had fought a long and hard campaign against the British army, the Royal Irish Constabulary, the Black and Tans and the RIC Auxiliaries and had brought the British military machine in Ireland to a standstill. On 11 July 1921, a truce had come into effect between the IRA and British forces. Five months later, on 5 December 1921, a peace treaty had been signed between the British government and representatives of the rebel Irish government. Now, in 1922, British forces were slowly being withdrawn from their barracks in the south of Ireland to be replaced by groups of Irishmen.

The final draft of the Treaty contained eighteen articles. Articles 1 and 2 gave the Irish Free State, comprising twenty-six of the thirty-two counties of Ireland, the same constitutional status as Canada, Australia and the other dominion states. Under Article 3, the British king would be represented in Ireland by a governor general appointed in the same way as the Canadian governor general. Article 4 of the Treaty set out the oath of allegiance to be taken by all members of the Irish parliament. It read:

> I ... do solemnly swear true faith and allegiance to the Constitution of the Irish Free State as by law established, and that I will be faithful to His Majesty King George V, his heirs and successors by law, in virtue of the common citizenship of Ireland with Great Britain and her adherence to and membership of the group of nations forming the British Commonwealth of Nations.

Article 5 covered the amount of the British war debt that would be paid by the Irish Free State. Article 6 dealt with defence and under its provisions the British military would have permanent naval bases at Cobh, Berehaven and Lough Swilly, and would be given additional bases and military facilities in times of war. Article 10 ensured that the Irish Free State would pay pensions to former British civil servants who had been stationed in Ireland. Pensions would also be paid to the RIC, with the exception of members of the force recruited in Britain. Articles 11 to 15 detailed the position of Northern Ireland.

In theory the Free State was to take over the functions of the British government for ruling the six counties under the Government of Ireland Act unless the unionist parliament at Stormont voted to remain within the United Kingdom. In that event the border between 'Northern' and 'Southern' Ireland would be drawn up by a boundary commission consisting of three members, one each appointed by the Free State, Northern Irish and British governments. Article 16 forbade either the Free State or Northern Irish governments to give special treatment to any religion. Finally the British government would hand over control of the twenty-six counties of Southern Ireland to a provisional government made up of existing Irish MPs.

The issue of whether to accept or reject this Treaty split Dáil Éireann – the rebel Irish government, Sinn Féin, the IRA, Cumann na mBan and all previously united republican organisations. Those who argued in favour of the Treaty claimed that while it did not deliver the republic they had struggled and suffered for since 1916, it was a fair compromise and realistically the most power and independence that they could get from the British government at the time. The Treaty guaranteed the removal of British forces from most of Ireland and that the British flag would no longer be flown over the war-weary populace in the south, many of whom saw it as a symbol of oppression at this time. Supporters of the Treaty claimed that the oath of allegiance to the British king was merely a formality and that they had forced the British negotiators to accept a very weak form of oath. At last the Irish people would have a government recognised by the British, their own army, state and flag. They would have control of their own economic affairs and the Free State would control its own courts, its own justice system and could establish its own police force.

Most of those who accepted the Treaty also felt that partition of Northern Ireland was merely a temporary measure and that the boundary commission would ultimately deliver so much territory to the Free State that the remaining area would be too small to be viable. This, they hoped, would result in the northern unionists taking the option to join the Free State, ultimately delivering a United Ireland. Many thought there was no alternative other than continuing the war with Britain, and they believed the Treaty would bring about a permanent peace. While the new Free State would not deliver them the ultimate freedom they longed for, it gave them the possibility of what Michael Collins called 'the freedom to achieve freedom'. According to Robert Barton, a member of the Irish government who had signed the Treaty:

> Collins looked upon the Treaty as being, as he said, a stepping stone to complete independence. He believed in accepting it, working it as far as it suited us and doing what has happened since, using it as a means of getting more.[3]

Opposing them, the republicans poured scorn on the Treaty and its supposed freedoms. They considered it a betrayal of everything they had fought for and an insult to the hundreds who had given their lives in that cause since 1916. They refused to swear an oath of loyalty to a foreign monarch and would rather continue the fight to become citizens of a fully independent Irish Republic than live as subjects of a foreign king within the British Empire. They regarded the establishment of the Free State and granting of dominion status as little more than a glorified form of Home Rule. They argued that the Irish Republic had been declared in 1916 and confirmed by the results of the 1918 general election, the establishment of Dáil Éireann and its ratification of the declaration of Independence in 1919.

To them the republic already existed and no treaty or government assembly could ever abolish the established right of the Irish people to complete independence. They had sworn allegiance to the republic and were prepared to die to defend it. They saw partition as a permanent political and social evil which would leave their northern comrades at the mercy of a hostile unionist population and British forces. They had no faith in a boundary commission and knew the partition of the six Ulster counties with the highest unionist majority, ensured that gerrymandering would be engrained in Northern Ireland for years to come and that a unionist government would always be returned; a government certain to reject any plans for Irish unification. They saw partition as an unnatural division of Ireland pandering to a unionist minority – not just a minority within Ireland but a minority within the nine counties of Ulster as well. Republicans could also not stomach the fact that Irish taxpayers were now expected to pay the pensions of RIC and Irish recruits to the Black and Tans, who had terrorised the Irish people at the behest of a foreign government.

The Treaty represented a compromise for the British that would allow them to end their involvement in an unpopular war which was costing the state up to £20 million a year, as well as damaging their international reputation. They needed a settlement that they could claim was a victory over the republicans, keeping Ireland as part of the British Empire, while at the same time allowing them to withdraw their forces from Ireland without losing face. The terms of the Treaty allowed them to achieve this.

During the Truce period Pádraig Ó Fathaigh, an IRA volunteer with the Mid Clare Brigade, had returned to his native Galway and foresaw that the question of accepting or rejecting the Treaty with Britain would lead to civil war:

> The Auxiliary officer Br - who shot Father Griffin spoke the truth when he said to Miss Walshe that there would be a slaughter of Sinn Féiners soon and when she said, 'That cannot be as ye are going', he replied, 'It's no joke, the Sinn Féiners will slaughter each other. It is all arranged and you will find that what I say is true.'[4]

On 7 January Dáil Éireann voted by sixty-four votes to fifty-seven in favour of the Treaty. After the vote de Valera resigned as president and republican TDs withdrew from the assembly in protest. De Valera was replaced by Arthur Griffith, who appointed a new cabinet with Michael Collins as minister for finance, Richard Mulcahy as minister for defence, William T. Cosgrave as minister for local government and Kevin O'Higgins as minister for economic affairs. Under the terms of the Treaty, the Irish Free State was to come into existence on 6 December 1922, the first anniversary of the signing of the Treaty. Until the Free State was established, the British government would hand over power in stages to a Provisional Government elected by the parliament of 'Southern Ireland' under the terms of the Government of Ireland Act. In reality the 'southern' parliament consisted of the members of the Dáil, including the four unionist TDs representing Trinity College who had refused to attend Dáil Éireann. The Provisional Government met a week later on 14 January 1922 and elected Michael Collins as its chairman.

Following the Dáil vote on the Treaty, senior IRA officers who opposed the Treaty's acceptance and its implementation held a series of talks. As a result of these Liam Lynch proposed that the IRA would revert to its original status prior to 1919, as an army of committed unpaid volunteers under the control of an elected executive. The entire IRA would be represented on this executive, regardless of their views on the Treaty. This would have two main results. Firstly it would halt the influx of 'Trucileers', men who had swollen the ranks of the IRA after the Truce, either in hope of financial gain now that some IRA members were being paid as soldiers in a semi-professional army, or who sought to bask in the glory of the organisation even though they had played no part in the fight against the British. Secondly it would refocus the IRA on maintaining army unity and hopefully find a way of securing a fully independent Irish Republic. In order to make this change a convention had to be held for the election of an executive as soon as possible. This convention would also give the membership of the IRA a chance to ratify or reject the Treaty. With the exception of the IRA's 4th Northern Division under the command of Frank Aiken, who had adopted a neutral stance, all IRA units agreed to hold a convention in March. In addition Richard Mulcahy, minister for defence in the Provisional Government, gave a personal assurance that the existing Irish army, both the anti-Treaty units that continued as the Irish Republican Army and the pro-Treaty units that were beginning to form the new Free State army, would be maintained for the defence of the Irish Republic.

With the formation of the Provisional Government in January, the British army began to withdraw from their barracks throughout the twenty-six counties. Some returned home to Britain, while others were transferred north across the border to reinforce the unionist government. As the British forces withdrew, their former barracks were taken over by both pro-Treaty and anti-Treaty units of the IRA. Each IRA unit moved into the evacuated barracks in their area regardless of their political loyalties on the issue of the Treaty. The first barracks to be evacuated by the British was Beggars Bush in Dublin, which was taken over by pro-Treaty members of the Dublin Brigade IRA. The Provisional Government wanted to make sure that the men looked well for the occasion and sent their pro-Treaty troops to the Co-Op Tailors in Abbey Street to be fitted for new green uniforms. The political split between the pro-Treaty and anti-Treaty IRA units became clearly visible with the pro-Treaty men wearing their new green uniforms. The British army handed over Beggars Bush barracks to the Dublin Brigade of the Free State army on 31 January 1922. As the British soldiers withdrew, a British army officer, Lieutenant Bevin, was shot at by an IRA sniper as he was riding a motor cycle. The IRA sniper's bullet passed through his jacket but he was not injured. This incident made it clear that the republicans did not regard the Treaty as a final settlement with the British.

Tensions grew between the IRA and the new Free State army, leading to armed clashes, as both jostled to take the military advantage. The competition to take over local barracks as the British army and RIC withdrew, became part of this struggle all over the country.

CHAPTER 2

EARLY HOSTILITIES
IN LIMERICK

In Limerick city on 16 February, the IRA held up two Black and Tans, Constables Williams and Harding, at Pery Square and took their revolvers. Two days later, on 18 February, Liam Forde, commandant of the Mid Limerick Brigade, issued a proclamation denouncing the Treaty and repudiating the authority of Michael Collins, Richard Mulcahy, and the other members of the IRA's headquarters staff in Dublin who supported the Treaty, and declared his brigade independent of headquarters' control and loyal to the Irish Republic:

> This republic has been ratified by the people of Ireland and members of the IRA were sworn to maintain it. The aims of

the head of the army and the majority of the GHQ staff are now unquestionably to subvert the republic and to support the Provisional Government, and to make possible the establishment of the Irish Free State. We therefore declare that we no longer recognise the authority of the head of the army and renew our allegiance to the existing Irish Republic. We are confident that in this stand we will have the support of all units of the IRA and of every loyal citizen of the Irish Republic.[5]

On the same day, the IRA's South Tipperary Brigade issued a similar proclamation. In response Richard Mulcahy ordered Commandant General Michael Brennan and Free State troops from the 1st Western Division in East Clare and South Galway to enter Limerick city and take over the military barracks that the British army was due to evacuate. Officially the Provisional Government's policy was for the local force to take over all evacuated British army barracks in their brigade area regardless of whether they were IRA or Free State army. However Limerick city was regarded as a key military position – it had been strongly garrisoned by British forces who had used it as a base during the War of Independence to dominate large parts of counties Clare, Limerick and Tipperary. Its position spanning the Shannon meant that it linked control of Munster and the western coast. If the IRA took military control of the city they would be able to consolidate their position in the south and west. This would have left Commandant Seán MacEoin and

Michael Brennan's Free State troops in Clare, Galway and the midlands surrounded by IRA brigades, and dangerously isolated from the rest of the Free State forces, except for the East Limerick Brigade and a few battalions of the Mid Limerick Brigade who also supported the Treaty.

Alternatively, if the Free State gained control of the city they would be able to cut off communications between the IRA in Connacht and Munster and could use the city as a base for mounting attacks on both of these areas. So Richard Mulcahy broke from the Provisional Government's usual policy and ordered pro-Treaty troops into Limerick.

On 23 February the RIC evacuated the city's five police barracks. Many of the Black and Tans and Auxiliaries who had been stationed there changed into civilian clothes, and enjoyed a few hasty drinks before setting to work gathering up their belongings and removing the RIC station plates and other British emblems from the front of the buildings to take home as souvenirs. The men who had evacuated the barracks celebrated the historic occasion with a few more drinks and one party made an unsteady march along Clare Street firing shots in the air from their revolvers in celebration. IRA Volunteer Mossie Hartnet was returning from a training camp when he encountered them at Limerick Station:

> We arrived at Limerick Railway Station carrying rifles and
> equipment and we were standing there awaiting the train

to Tralee, when out of the blue and to our discomfiture and dismay about one hundred or so Black and Tans ran all over the place, jumping gates, shouting, whistling and acting like a mob bent on destruction. When they saw us they gathered around us – some shouted, 'Here are the bloody Shinners!'

'Here are some of the invisible army!'

This was the first time we had met any of our opponents; before this we could never see them. Some shook us by the hand and said that at least they had met some IRA men and could tell their friends about it. Some said that they only wanted pay given them and that only necessity forced them to be in Ireland. Some were from as far away as Canada. They looked unkempt, unshaven, some under the influence of drink and acted in the most unruly manner. The stationmaster was distracted by their behaviour and was frantic with fear. In his distress he appealed to us for help, but it was like asking the blind to help the blind, as we were worried ourselves. The arrival of a large party of the old RIC police force soon calmed the atmosphere and all was well again to our relief.[6]

The IRA had not been notified of the evacuations by the British and by this time Brennan had already marched his Free State troops into the city unnoticed, along the railway line. The first RIC barracks evacuated was in William Street and, shortly after the last of its occupants left, it was taken over by Captain F.J. O'Shaughnessy of the Free State army and a tricolour flag of green, white and orange was set flying from one of the upper windows. He quickly spread his other troops throughout the city and took possession of the RIC barracks in Mary Street. That evening the garrison of the Royal Welch Fusiliers at King John's Castle vacated the barracks there and were provided with motor transport to Dublin for evacuation. At 5.30 p.m. a party of seventy fully armed Free State soldiers arrived from Ennis by train to reinforce Brennan's garrison in Limerick. Michael Brennan took command of these men and marched them through the streets to the Castle. That night they were reinforced by a further forty unarmed Free State soldiers who also arrived from Ennis.

The entry of Michael Brennan's Free State units to Limerick city was the first time during the British withdrawal that one army division had been ordered into another's divisional area and the tension between Free State forces and the local IRA created a powder keg in Limerick, ready to explode and ignite civil war. Limerick city was part of the area controlled by the IRA's 2nd Southern Division under Ernie O'Malley's command. As soon as the Mid Limerick Brigade of the IRA discovered that Michael Brennan's Free State troops had occupied barracks, they sent a courier with word to O'Malley to come and take control of the situation.

The local IRA volunteers were angered by the invasion of what they saw as their territory by 'outsiders'. In response to this, Captain John Hurley, former quartermaster of the IRA's Mid Limerick Brigade, and leader of a minority from the brigade who supported the Treaty, attempted to organise his own Free State force of Limerick men to take over the barracks evacuated by the British. Hurley's hope was that if Brennan was willing to hand over these positions to his men, they would be a more acceptable body of Free State troops than the 'outsiders' from Clare. However, before Hurley could implement his plan he was arrested by another group of outsiders – IRA men from Cork and Tipperary who had come to reinforce the Limerick republicans. In protest Hurley immediately began a hunger strike.

A week later, on 1 March, the Oxfordshire and Buckinghamshire Light Infantry handed over control of the Strand barracks to Captain F.J. O'Shaughnessy and moved to their temporary accommodation in the city's Ordnance barracks. The following night Ernie O'Malley arrived in Limerick with IRA volunteers from the 2nd Southern Division in response to the Mid Limerick Brigade's appeal for reinforcements. On 7 March, IRA columns from Kilkenny and Galway marched on Limerick, as did a contingent of 200 more Free State soldiers from Clare who made their way to the Castle barracks. A second force of Free State troops from East Limerick reached the city the same night to reinforce the garrison in William Street police barracks.

The same day Stephen O'Mara, the Sinn Féin mayor of Limerick and an influential republican, managed to get both sides talking, but his efforts to work out a solution to the growing tensions failed. Arthur Griffith remained intransigent in his demand that the IRA should withdraw from the city before any settlement could be reached, so the Free State troops had little room to manoeuvre at this point. In response the mayor said that he 'almost thought it would be better to burn the barracks than to risk a continuation of the situation'.[7] Neither Michael Brennan's nor Ernie O'Malley's forces were prepared to concede control of the city and, as the situation grew more fraught, the outbreak of fighting in Limerick seemed inevitable.

The situation escalated as both the IRA and Free State troops started to commandeer hotels and other large buildings in the city as barracks. A small force of British soldiers remained in the Ordnance and New barracks awaiting the order to withdraw – but they were uncertain of who they should hand these barracks over to when that order came. Amongst them was a British officer with the Oxfordshire and Buckinghamshire Light Infantry who described the newly arrived IRA units as '… a nondescript sort of party, fairly well armed, and in the matter of transport their motto seemed to be "To every man his own Ford".'[8]

O'Malley describes the situation in Limerick at this point:

Extra Mulcahyites [Free State troops] arrived. We marched and counter marched to give the appearance of having more men than were actually there. Supplies of landmines had been prepared, the city had been surveyed and supplies of sand, sandbags and barbed wire had been commandeered … The British armoured cars patrolled up and down, as did the armoured cars from the Castle barracks.[9]

By now the situation was reaching boiling point as IRA units were heading for the city from surrounding counties, including members of the 3rd West Cork Brigade led by Tom Barry. Liam Forde, the commandant of the Mid Limerick Brigade, told O'Malley that one of the Free State soldiers stationed in the Castle barracks, a former member of the IRA's Mid Clare Brigade, had approached the IRA offering to supply them with information about the strength of the barracks garrison and O'Malley arranged to interview him:

Late that night a tall, uniformed officer with a soft green uniform cap came to the house.

'I remember meeting you in 1919,' he said, 'in Mid Clare.'

I did not remember his face. I talked casually whilst I tried to remember the last occasion I had met him but I could not.

'We thought we were going to Dublin to Beggars Bush barracks first,' he said, 'then we found ourselves in the Castle barracks here. Some of us did not like coming into your area, the others did not mind. They say you are rebels and General Headquarters is going to have its authority recognised in Limerick.'

'We don't want trouble,' I said, 'but the troops in the Castle and Strand barracks will have to leave.'

I asked for the names of the Dublin officers. He gave them to me. I enquired about strengths. He told me the position of the sentries, of the machine-gun posts, the strength of the guard-room, the situation of the officers' quarters. He seemed anxious to give information. He drew rough sketches for me.

'Are you willing to help?' I asked.

'I am,' he replied, 'I'm a Republican.'

'How do you return to the barracks?'

'I have late leave. I knock at the front gate; one of the sentries opens it. I flash a light from my lamp when I get inside, tell my name and then walk across to my room.'

'Are you willing to get late leave tomorrow night? I will have some men here. We will follow you in the gate, gag the sentries, hold up the guardroom and rush the officers' quarters. We don't want any shooting.'

'All right,' he said 'I'll do that,' and he left the room.

I knew the Dublin officers, Slattery, Stapleton and Kehoe. They had been members of Collins' intelligence squad.

'They will fight,' said the Brigadier [Liam Forde]. 'We will have to manage the sentries and the guardroom very quickly, and then lead the men to the officers' rooms. Once we have them prisoners, there will be little trouble with the officers of the men.'

'Whether there's shooting or not, the Free State army is not going to seize a portion of my area,' I said. 'It will have to be confronted sometime. Trouble might as well begin in this division.'[10]

The same night the Limerick city units of the IRA raided the homes of their former comrades who had joined the Free

State army and took their weapons. O'Malley sent a dispatch to Seamus Robinson and the 3rd Tipperary Brigade of the IRA requesting fifty fully armed IRA volunteers to take part in the attack on the barracks the following evening. IRA volunteers from Limerick would be ready to guide them to the rendezvous point for the raid. While O'Malley was busy mobilising his forces for the raid, Limerick city was quickly becoming a rallying point for the IRA in their campaign against the Treaty. By now Tom Barry had arrived in the city, leading a detachment of IRA volunteers from the 1st Southern Division in Cork and individual IRA units were marching on Limerick ready to fight the Free State troops. Meanwhile O'Malley was planning the IRA's attack:

We had studied the rough sketches before we approached the barracks. We identified the officers' quarters and other buildings. We again visited the narrow by-lanes.

'This would be a good place to keep our men while we're waiting in the night for the Clare officer,' I thought. 'There are not many houses here.'

It was a small lane, deep in mud; puddles of water lay where the roadway had sunk. We crossed the river by the swivel bridge near the boat club and looked at the Strand barracks, which was in view of the Castle; then we returned to the house we had been staying in off the Tipperary road. We checked off the imaginary men for the raid. Ourselves, two to hold up the sentries, two men to tie them up; six men for the guardroom; eight for the officers' quarters, and ourselves, twelve men for the men's quarters; a reserve of ten men to remain near the guardroom and twenty more men to cover the outside approaches: total sixty … At ten o'clock that night the Tipperary force had arrived. It had numerous cars, lorries, Crossley Tenders, a Lewis gun and seventy men. The transport was placed in a small bohereen off the main road. A guard was mounted. It was raining; the wind lashed our faces as we detailed off the men and explained what we had to do. We moved quietly through the muddy lanes in groups; heavy coats; the darkness and the rain hiding our weapons. There were few people out of doors. We reached the lane near the barracks. After the men had been arranged in order of entry we laid up against a wall and tried to shelter. The Clare officer was due to arrive at 11.30 pm. We waited; no officer. Twelve o'clock; he had not appeared. Perhaps he had been delayed we thought. We waited until one o'clock. Then thoroughly wet and in bad humour, we moved back to the Tipperary road.

'He must have funked it,' one of us said.

'We're here now,' I said. 'We can't surprise the barracks. We'd better occupy some buildings and wait till morning.'[11]

O'Malley's men took control of St Joseph's asylum that night. The next morning he placed IRA volunteers in the Royal George and Glentworth Hotels using them as makeshift barracks. At midday he telephoned the Castle barracks to arrange a meeting with the leaders of the Free State troops stationed there:

I was told to come over at once as they would like to talk to us. Another officer and I walked across the barracks' yard and were met by Slattery, Stapleton and Kehoe. They brought us to a room overlooking the yard.

'Well,' said Slattery, 'we were expecting you earlier but you did not come,' and he smiled.

I wondered if he was referring to our raid. Perhaps the officer had given information.

'I want you to leave the city … You have no authority to enter the divisional area … I'm delivering an ultimatum … I want these officers to leave Limerick … I will give you twelve hours notice prior to hostilities,' I said to Slattery, then we walked back to our headquarters at the Glentworth.[12]

O'Malley then wrote to Rory O'Connor in Dublin, the new chairman of the IRA council, on 9 March requesting a team of IRA engineers with explosives to be sent to Limerick for an attack on the Castle. O'Malley stated that his men: 'Will be ready to knock the hell out of the others in two or three days time.'[13] However, O'Connor turned down his request in an attempt to halt the slide into civil war. O'Malley protested that if the IRA did not act in Limerick, the Free State army would occupy all the important military barracks in Dublin, Athlone and Limerick and would have the military advantage. In short, the Free State army would have won the war before it even began. But without O'Connor's approval, engineers and explosives, O'Malley's attack on the

Free State-held barracks in Limerick was bound to fail and so he was forced to abandon the idea.

Tom Kelliher, one of the leaders of the 3rd West Cork Brigade, was as frustrated as O'Malley with the lack of action by the IRA, which was letting the military advantage slip from its grasp.

> Barry and the other leaders felt that the Free State element in Dublin should be disarmed, but they failed to move decisively until it was too late. I'll be very honest; our personnel were not up to the mark at all. In Limerick we had plenty of good fighters. The [Free] Staters were not numerous. Yet attacks were not pressed when they could have been … It's my personal opinion that Liam Lynch and Liam Deasy were simply not up to it, but neither were our headquarters' staff in Dublin. We were allowed to fragment in the countryside when we could have throttled the Staters in the early months of 1922.[14]

Despite the lack of decisive orders, combatants continued to pour into the city and battle lines were drawn as the Free State troops took control of the Union Workhouse and Shannon Rowing Club while the republicans commandeered the courthouse and custom house. Michael Brennan's troops in Limerick city were now facing a formidable fighting force of the most battle-hardened IRA units from the War of Independence, along with the leaders who had inflicted the heaviest losses on the British during that war. These included Tom Barry and Tom Hales, 3rd West Cork Brigade, Seán Moylan and the 2nd North Cork Brigade, Peadar O'Loughlin and the Mid Clare Brigade, Dinny Lacey's Flying Column from Tipperary and a section of the 2nd Western Division under the command of T. O'Gorman.

The situation in Limerick was rapidly turning into a major challenge to the authority of the Provisional Government and Arthur Griffith urged the Free State army commanders to attack the IRA's positions and take control of the entire city, no matter what the implications. Initially he was supported by Michael Collins, but Richard Mulcahy vetoed the suggestion, pointing out that the Free State army was not yet well enough armed or equipped for war. Instead Griffith issued the following statement:

> The situation in Limerick is largely the outcome of incitement to indiscipline indulged in, or connived at, by some of Mr de Valera's supporters … This negation of national authority can under no circumstances be acquiesced to.[15]

In private Griffith was extremely angry and declared to Richard Mulcahy that if the Free State didn't face down the IRA and take control of the city they would go down as 'the greatest poltroons in Irish history'.[16] However, the IRA in the city and throughout the country by now seemed to hold the military advantage and Richard Mulcahy ruled out any prospect of a Free State attack when he received Michael

Brennan's report on the strength of the IRA in Limerick city:

> There are 800 mutineers [IRA volunteers] here at present all armed with rifles and most of them with revolvers also. They have a splendid transport service – we have practically none … [Seamus] Robinson [3rd Tipperary Brigade IRA] told me yesterday that they propose putting 3,000 or 4,000 men here. I propose cutting down my garrison here but increasing my reserves outside … As it is a foregone conclusion that the mutineers will be able to lock us in, I propose cutting down the Limerick garrison to 500 reliable men … Some of my men have too many associations with the mutineers to be properly reliable, hence my anxiety to get 100 good men from McKeown [MacEoin]. The 3rd Southern [Division] is too near things to be thoroughly reliable.[17]

Mulcahy's original plan of taking control of Limerick city by occupying barracks and other positions with Free State troops, had failed. The only option left to him other than open conflict, which the Free State army would almost certainly lose, was to open negotiations with the IRA. This way he could avoid open warfare until his troops were in a stronger military position and could mount a military offensive at a time of the Free State government's choosing.

On 10 March Liam Lynch, the commander of the 1st Southern Division of the IRA, and Oscar Traynor, Commander of the Dublin Brigade of the IRA, were called to a meeting at the Free State army's new headquarters at Beggars Bush barracks, Dublin, arranged by Stephen O'Mara. They met Michael Collins, Richard Mulcahy and Eoin O'Duffy in an effort the calm the situation in Limerick. Eventually an agreement was reached. The remaining military barracks in the city still occupied by the British army would be handed over to Limerick Corporation. The Strand and Castle barracks were to be garrisoned by a force of local IRA volunteers from the Mid Limerick Brigade and all other IRA units would be withdrawn from the city. The former RIC barracks in the city would be evacuated by Brennan's Free State troops, who would withdraw back to their own divisional area in East Clare and Galway. The police barracks would be handed over to Limerick Corporation and would be occupied by a small civilian maintenance crew who would report to Liam Lynch's command. However, as a concession to the Free State, William Street police barracks would be manned by a token force of Free State soldiers under General William R.E. Murphy's command. After this meeting Lynch and Traynor travelled to Limerick to convince O'Malley and Barry to accept the agreement reached. Oscar Traynor later recalled how high tensions were running on both sides and how close the situation had come to sparking a civil war:

> In King John's Castle we saw [Michael] Brennan who tried to bluster as he said he was going to fight and he was puffed out in his uniform like a peacock. ... We had an awful job with

> [Tom] Barry … We saw fellows lying in numbers with rifles sticking out. … We were successful in getting people to call it off. Eventually they marched off singing and carrying their guns. We had to try and impress on Barry that there would be fighting at some time.[18]

Brennan was enraged that, having been ordered to march his men into the city and risk fighting a much larger IRA force, he was now being ordered to withdraw his troops. He felt that he had been forced into a humiliating personal retreat. He travelled to Dublin immediately after receiving news of the agreement to evacuate the Free State army and demanded to see Collins, to whom he presented a letter of resignation. Collins was angered when Brennan confronted him: 'So you're going too! The rats leaving the ship. Well, go on. Clear out! Leave it all to me. You're all the same, you fellows, putting your bloody vanity ahead of the good of the country.'[19] Collins continued to berate him in a similar fashion for a further ten minutes until Brennan relented and withdrew his resignation.

Even though fighting in Limerick had been avoided for the time being, Rory O'Connor, IRA Director of Engineering, made it clear in a letter to the IRA's Director of Publicity, Erskine Childers, on 11 March that the IRA was still prepared to fight to defend the Irish Republic:

> The matter is settled at this end. If the Limerick officers accept this, the whole incident is closed. If it has not been accepted in

Limerick you may take it for certain that there will be no further negotiations, and in fact fighting on the lines decided upon will have already commenced by the time you receive this note.[20]

One incident, however, indicated that while an accord had been reached for the present, relations between the two sides were by no means friendly. Richard Mulcahy had sent the first armoured car that the British government had handed over to the Free State, a Rolls Royce, to the John's Street police station in Limerick, via Templemore, to add to the Free State army's firepower in the city. The car was under the command of Captain Bill Stapleton and manned by a crew of four – two Free State soldiers and two Black and Tans who had been seconded to the Free State army to train the others on how to handle the vehicle. Now that the situation in Limerick had stabilised, the armoured car and its crew was ordered to head back to Dublin. On their journey into Limerick, the armoured car's crew had called into Templemore barracks where they were greeted with great hospitality by the garrison and treated to a few pints of stout. Expecting an equally warm welcome on their return journey to Dublin, they stopped at Templemore again. But this time as soon as they arrived they were immediately surrounded by armed men and forced to surrender.[21] Since they had last visited, the Templemore garrison had switched its allegiance from the Free State to the Republic and Captain Stapleton and his crew were taken prisoner having just delivered to the IRA its first armoured car!

This was a rather undignified end to a mission that had not gone entirely smoothly for Captain Stapleton. He had already been ambushed on 2 March by two young IRA volunteers, who wounded him in the hand as he entered a hotel on Thomas Street in Limerick city before making off with his revolver.

Stapleton and the two other Free State soldiers captured in Templemore were released shortly afterwards. The two captured Black and Tans were held for a further two days before being released – but not before the local IRA had publicised the fact that the hated Black and Tans were providing assistance to the Free State army. The armoured car was later sabotaged by two Free State soldiers who managed to sneak into Templemore barracks and remove a number of parts from the car's engine.

The Limerick situation had proved a major embarrassment to the Free State government's authority and Collins wrote to Winston Churchill requesting that he stop the British evacuation of the New and Ordnance barracks until the situation was more favourable from the Free State army's perspective. Churchill refused and replied on the 14 March:

> You seem to have liquidated the Limerick situation in one way or another. No doubt you know your own business best, and thank God you have got to manage it and not me. An adverse decision by the convention of the Irish Republican Army (so-called) would, however, be a very grave event at the present juncture. I presume you are quite sure there is no danger of this.[22]

CHAPTER 3

THE OUTBREAK
OF THE CIVIL WAR

The exceptionally tense atmosphere caused by the situation in Limerick and the fact that 70 to 80 per cent of the IRA was against the Treaty, led Minister for Defence Richard Mulcahy to fear that if the IRA convention was held, it might lead to the creation of a military dictatorship. Furthermore, the Free State army was still recruiting and awaiting further supplies of weapons from the British and was not yet in a position to challenge the might of the IRA. As a result, the Provisional Government decided on 15 March to ban the IRA army convention. However, Liam Lynch, Rory O'Connor and the other anti-Treaty IRA officers were determined to go ahead with the convention in defiance of the Provisional Government and the IRA's leaders took it upon themselves to call the convention for 26 March.

In accordance with the arrangement reached in Dublin, the remaining 500 British troops evacuated Limerick city on 21 March. That morning the Royal Army Service Corps and Mechanical Transport Corps climbed onto their Crossley Tender lorries and quietly departed for the Curragh. However, the remaining British soldiers from the Royal Welch Fusiliers and the Oxfordshire and Buckinghamshire Light Infantry left the city with more pomp and ceremony. They each marched to Limerick railway station from the New and Ordnance barracks respectively, led by their regimental bands and colour parties flying their regimental flags. They were met by a small group of unionists consisting mostly of young women, some waving British flags, as they boarded their trains for the Curragh. Within a few days the IRA had moved into their former barracks. Limerick city was now firmly in the hands of the republicans.

On 26 March the IRA convention of predominantly anti-Treaty IRA delegates met in the Mansion House, Dublin, with 223 delegates present representing fifty-two of the seventy-three IRA brigades throughout the country, or about 75 per cent of the IRA's volunteers. The convention passed a resolution that the army 'shall be maintained as the army of the Irish Republic under an executive appointed by the convention'. A temporary executive of sixteen was elected, headed by Liam Lynch, who had been made IRA chief-of-staff at the convention, and including Rory O'Connor, Liam Mellows, Liam Deasy and Ernie O'Malley, to control the IRA and replace the pro-Treaty former IRA commanders at general headquarters, like Collins and Mulcahy. The IRA executive established its headquarters at Barry's Hotel in Gardiner's Row, Dublin. The convention was adjourned until 9 April when a new constitution was to be discussed. It was now abundantly clear that the majority of the IRA was opposed to the Treaty and prepared to oppose it by force if necessary.

This opposition was made clear, as the IRA continued to train and re-arm for war. On 30 March six British soldiers travelling by train from Cork to Dublin for demobilisation, were disarmed and kidnapped by the IRA at Limerick Junction. On the evening of Sunday 2 April, 1922, seventeen-year-old Thomas Slattery of Gerald Griffin Street, a member of Na Fianna Éireann, the republican boy scouts, who supported and fought with the IRA during the War of Independence, was on a training exercise with Na Fianna when the revolver he was using malfunctioned. As he attempted to fix it, the gun went off accidentally and he was shot through the stomach. He was rushed to the County Infirmary where he was treated, but died early the following morning. He was buried in Mount Saint Lawrence Cemetery on Tuesday 5 April:

> The cortège was of large dimensions. Some companies of the
> deceased's comrades in the Fianna marched in military order.

A firing party of the IRA was in attendance, and a volley was fired over the grave and the 'Last Post' sounded.[23]

Tragically there was a second accidental shooting in the city less than a week later. On the morning of Sunday 9 April, IRA Volunteer Michael O'Neill from Barrack Lane, Limerick, was on duty in the guardroom of the New barracks when one of his comrades accidentally fired their rifle, mortally wounding him. An ambulance was called to the barracks and O'Neill was rushed to Barrington's hospital. However, the bullet had passed through O'Neill's lungs and he died the following evening.

In February the former RIC barracks at Broadford had been taken over by Free State troops from the 1st Western Division. On Saturday 8 April, the barracks' garrison withdrew their allegiance from the Provisional Government and threw in their lot with the republicans. The following night Free State troops surrounded the barracks and demanded that the garrison inside surrender. When they refused, the Free State's soldiers attacked the barracks and re-captured it, except for one room occupied by William O'Brien and a few others. After a brief firefight the republicans realised that their situation was hopeless and agreed to end their resistance and leave the barracks after a ceasefire was arranged with the Free State troops. As O'Brien led his men out of the room carrying his revolver, the Free State soldiers attempted to disarm him by force. A struggle ensued and he was shot through the heart.

On 15 April, an explosion in a factory on Edward Street in Limerick, where the IRA was making grenades, killed Michael O'Connell from Boherbuoy. Three other IRA members were wounded in the blast. O'Connell was buried in Mount Saint Lawrence Cemetery. On 26 May IRA Captain Thomas McInerny died in Barrington's hospital from wounds received after his own revolver was discharged in an accident three weeks earlier. McInerny was the driver of the car that plunged off Ballykissane Pier in Kerry on Good Friday 1916, while on a mission to contact the *Aud*.

However, despite the fact that they were clearly arming themselves and training for the inevitable outbreak of hostilities, all was not well within the ranks of the anti-Treaty IRA. Internal divisions on the issue of army policy caused the IRA executive to split and Liam Lynch resigned as IRA chief-of-staff. He was replaced by Joe McKelvey.

The section of the IRA who supported McKelvey was deeply unhappy at Liam Lynch's on-going talks with Free State army leaders through which he was trying to secure Irish army unity by reuniting the pro- and anti-Treaty forces. They proposed instead a new IRA campaign against British forces in the six counties, led by such formidable republicans as Joe McKelvey, Rory O'Connor, Tom Barry, Ernie O'Malley and Liam Mellows. They commandeered a number of strategically placed buildings in Dublin including the Four Courts, the Ballast Office and the Masonic Hall in Molesworth Street, on 14 April. From these bases they began to stockpile supplies and commandeer vehicles for the proposed incursion into Northern Ireland. This was a direct challenge to the authority of the Provisional Government, but Michael Collins and the other Free State leaders ignored it.

Collins wanted to prevent the outbreak of civil war to allow recruitment and training for the new Free State army, which was composed mainly of former IRA men, raw recruits and ex-British army soldiers, to continue. Recruitment and training were proceeding at a rapid pace and just two months after its establishment, the army contained 8,000 properly armed and well paid professional troops. In addition to this, Desmond Fitzgerald, a member of the Provisional Government, had made a request on behalf of the Government that the six British army regiments recruited in Ireland be absorbed into the Free State army. This request was refused by the British government, but many former members of these regiments soon joined the Free State army when their regiments in the British army were disbanded. As professional soldiers their only realistic options for a paid military career in Ireland were now to join a new regiment in the British army and serve in Northern Ireland, or enlist in the Free State army.

Some who supported the Treaty later claimed that the Free State army was made up entirely of former IRA volunteers who had served in the War of Independence. Free Stater John Pinkman claimed in his memoirs:

> Anyone wishing to join the National Army had to have served in the volunteers and upon joining up was, in fact transferred from the IRA into the National Army.[24]

However, the Free State was prepared to use the experience of ex-British soldiers who had no IRA service, to mould the army into a professional fighting force. Some ex-British soldiers who were found to have served in Ireland during the War of Independence and then joined the Free State army, were immediately discharged upon discovery. However, Pinkman records that one ex-British officer who enlisted in the Free State army, Major James C. Fitzmaurice, ex-Royal Flying Corps, was guilty of mistreating republican prisoners in Cork during the Civil War, yet he remained in the Free State army and was later promoted to the rank of colonel.[25]

In the west the situation remained tense, and on 21 April the IRA held up a Dublin-bound train at Limerick Junction and arrested forty-four Free State army recruits en route to Beggars Bush barracks for training. The Free State recruits were taken under guard to Tipperary barracks but were released later that evening and escorted back to Limerick city by the IRA.

On 26 May, 150 newly trained Free State soldiers, mostly from Limerick, arrived in the city from Drogheda. They reported to Commandant General William R.E. Murphy at William Street police barracks. Murphy sent a third of his reinforcements to occupy Limerick prison and the Munster Fair Tavern. By commandeering the prison as a barracks, Murphy could establish a base of operations in the southeast of the city which was almost completely in republican hands. The building also had a strategic importance, as it was a large stone building which would be easy to defend, and was situated directly between the IRA outposts at the Ordnance barracks and St Joseph's asylum.

In the dead of night, fifty Free State soldiers marched up William Street from Murphy's headquarters in the police barracks to take control of the prison. They expected an attack from the IRA garrison in the Ordnance barracks, but it never came. Upon entering the prison itself they were greeted by an even bigger surprise. As they went from cell to cell reviewing and interrogating the prisoners, they came across a West African named Jack Monday. This came as quite a shock to the Free State soldiers who had never laid eyes on a black man before with the exception of statues of St Martin. Jack had arrived in Limerick working as a fitter on a ship in December 1921. As his boat was leaving port it followed maritime custom by hoisting the flag of the country from which it was departing. But instead of flying the British flag it flew the Irish tricolour. The ship was immediately boarded by a party of Black and Tans and a fight ensued during which Jack stabbed two of them. He had been imprisoned in Limerick prison ever since, without being sentenced. (At the suggestion of his liberators, who could find no fault against him, he joined the Transit Corps of the Free State army some time later and was stationed at Gormanstown camp until 1928. He was even supposed to have gone so far as to have changed his name to Irish at some stage, becoming 'Séan de Luain.')[26] Despite this blatant contravention of the agreement made between the IRA and the Free State officials in March, there was no reaction from the IRA in the city, many of whose members were still unwilling to fire the first shots in the conflict.

Surprisingly it was to be an incident largely unrelated to the Treaty that was to set off an escalation in hostilities between the pro- and anti-Treaty forces. On 22 June, Sir Henry Wilson, the Northern Ireland government's advisor on security, was assassinated in London by two IRA members, Reginald Dunne and Joseph O'Sullivan, on the orders of Collins. This was in retaliation to Wilson's role in the War of Independence and his active encouragement of sectarian violence in Belfast. During the War of Independence, Wilson had called for the official courts-martial and execution of captured IRA volunteers. In the six months between January and June 1922, 171 Catholics and 93 Protestants were killed during sectarian rioting in the six counties. The unionist government of Northern Ireland introduced the 'Special Powers Act' in April 1922. This act was used to increase the number of 'B Specials', a largely sectarian part-time police force in the six counties, by recruiting former UVF members. The number of British army soldiers in Northern Ireland was also rapidly increased and they were placed under Wilson's command. He used these forces largely against the northern republican and Catholic communities.

Both of Wilson's assassins were former members of the British army. They were captured because O'Sullivan, who had lost a leg at Ypres during the First World War, could only hobble away after the shooting and Dunne refused to leave him. The British government was outraged by Wilson's killing and automatically assumed that Rory O'Connor and the IRA command in the Four Courts were responsible. Ernie O'Malley strenuously rejected this claim and laid the blame on Michael Collins:

We believed that Wilson had been shot through instructions from the Irish Republican Brotherhood, that is through Collins, O'Hegarty and Mulcahy who were members of the supreme council. Two of Collins' trusted men had been in London before the shooting took place. Arthur Griffith, who was not connected with the IRB, sent a message of sympathy to King George and Wilson's family. The English accused Four Courts staff of instigating the shooting. The Four Courts officers had nothing to do with it ... The motive of the crime was not apparent. Perhaps Collins may have wished to appease some of the northern officers who were members of the IRB and who required some assurance other than a promise of arms. The establishment of a Free State would cut them off from the remainder of the country. Some of them believed that he had deserted them, others he had promised arms to.[27]

In April Churchill had drawn up plans for the British government's 'Irish Situation Committee' to deal with any IRA armed coup or uprising in Dublin. After Wilson's assassination, the British government sent orders on 24 June to General Macready, who commanded the remaining British forces in Dublin, to put those plans into effect and mount an attack on the Four Courts the following day. Such an action would undoubtedly have restarted the war between the British forces and the IRA. Macready discussed the details with General Boyd and was unhappy about the prospect of attacking the Four Courts in the fear that it would unite the Free State army and the IRA against the British. That evening Macready sent Colonel Brind to London with a letter arguing against the attack.[28] The next day, before Macready could begin the attack, Churchill withdrew the order and instead publicly demanded that Michael Collins and the Free State government take action against the IRA in the Four Courts.

On 27 June, an IRA unit from the republican garrison in the Four Courts began commandeering motor vehicles to transport weapons northwards for an attack on the British forces in the six counties in order to re-start the war against the British. Leo Henderson, the IRA officer leading this unit, was arrested by the Free State army. In retaliation

and in the hope of securing his release, the IRA arrested
J.J. O'Connell, the deputy chief-of-staff of the Free State
army. O'Connell's arrest gave Michael Collins the excuse he
needed to attack the Four Courts and allow him to claim
that he was acting on his own initiative rather than following
the British government's orders. On 28 June, the Free State
army acting on Collins' orders and armed with field artillery
guns borrowed from the British army, issued an ultimatum
to Joe McKelvey and to the IRA inside the Four Courts to
leave the building by four o'clock that morning and surrender
to the Free State troops outside. Churchill had also offered
Collins the RAF, sporting Irish colours, to bomb the Four
Courts from the air, but this offer was politely refused.[29]

Paddy O'Brien, commander of the Four Courts garrison,
and Oscar Traynor, leader of the IRA's Dublin Brigade, had
drawn up a plan to attack the Free State army's positions
from the rear and wear them down with constant sniping.[30]
However, this plan was vetoed by the IRA executive who did
not want to be the first to open fire. This meant that the Free
State troops could surround the Four Courts in preparation
for the attack without any interference. With this threat of
action against their colleagues in the Four Courts, there was
a re-unification between the Lynch and McKelvey factions
of the IRA.

The IRA in the Four Courts ignored the Free State
ultimatum. Ernie O'Malley was inside the building with Rory
O'Connor when the Free State army's deadline arrived:

'Time's up,' said Rory, and as he spoke a machine-gun from outside echoed across the night, to be answered by a shout from each of our sections. A heavy boom came next, and we knew artillery was being used; the crash of an eighteen-pound shell announced that those who stood in arms for an independent Ireland were to be attacked by some of their former comrades.[31]

After months of careful negotiations and efforts to avoid open conflict, the first shots in the inevitable civil war had finally been fired.

The officers and men of the Oxfordshire and Buckinghamshire Light Infantry, who had recently evacuated Limerick city, watched the shelling of the Four Courts with glee as their former Irish foes started tearing each other apart:

Standing as it does, well above the surrounding houses, the North Dublin Union can be recommended to visitors to Dublin as a most suitable position from which to view any fracas that might be going on at the time. We found it excellent for this purpose, and during the whole of the so-called battle of the Four Courts, the windows and fire escapes were thronged with sightseers. This battle was perhaps the most humorous of the many humorous incidents which we witnessed in Ireland. The republican bravoes, under the leadership of one Rory O'Connor, had seized the Four Courts. This was understood to be a silent protest against the Free State party for keeping to themselves all the barracks handed over by the British government, such conduct being considered a gross breach of etiquette towards old comrades ...[32]

Liam Lynch was in the Clarence Hotel when the attack on the Four Courts started and he immediately set out for Limerick to take command of the situation there. He believed that the Dublin IRA was in control of the situation and was following an IRA executive decision that Southern Division officers should return to Munster to take up command of their divisions, which were the IRA's most experienced and effective units. Lynch's main role was to set up IRA headquarters in Limerick, the most strategically important city in the conflict after Dublin.[33] On the following day, 29 June, Lynch set up his headquarters in the New barracks in Limerick and assumed command again as IRA chief-of-staff from McKelvey, who was trapped inside the Four Courts.

As the Free State army's attack on the Four Courts was beginning in Dublin, IRA volunteers from the New barracks in Limerick city, warned of the inevitable outbreak of fighting, had occupied the YMCA hall and the Mechanics Institute at the rear of the barracks on Barrington Street, and began sandbagging them for defence. The buildings were immediately surrounded by Free State soldiers under Commandant Murphy's command and he ordered the republicans inside to leave the buildings or be forced out. Father Murphy, OSA, intervened and, acting as an intermediary between the two groups, managed to secure an agreement that the IRA would withdraw back to their barracks if the Free State soldiers also withdrew. Later that night, at 11.30 p.m., a man apparently the worse for wear with drink, carrying a German Mauser rifle, opened fire on the few Free State soldiers stationed at William Street police barracks, all the time shouting 'Up the Rebels!' and other republican slogans. He was rushed and disarmed by the barracks guard, who then allowed him to return home to sleep it off, escorted by a group of female relatives.

The IRA continued to fight on in Dublin city for another week, but bad communications, their overly defensive tactics and the superior Free State weaponry and firepower supplied by the British government, meant that a republican defeat in the city was inevitable. In the week's fighting sixty-five people were killed in Dublin and between three and four million pounds worth of damage had been caused. In a desperate effort to arrange a ceasefire and stop the fighting from spreading throughout the country, Maud Gonne MacBride led a delegation of female republicans, suffragettes, socialists and trade unionists to talk to Oscar Traynor, O/C of the IRA's Dublin Brigade, and Arthur Griffith in an effort to open peace talks. Maud Gonne later claimed that 'as women on whom the misery of civil war would fall, that we had a right to be heard'. However, Griffith refused to take the women seriously or accept any terms for a ceasefire, and expressed his desire to follow the Free State's campaign through to the bitter end by stating: 'We are now a government and we have to keep order.'[34]

As the Civil War began, the IRA held the military advantage over the Free State army, having superior numbers outside Dublin with a total fighting strength throughout Ireland of approximately 12,900 volunteers, mostly experienced veterans of the war against the British, motivated by republican ideals and armed with 6,780 rifles. In addition the republicans had almost complete control of Munster and most of the west coast, where each IRA unit was deeply connected with the local area and its people, benefiting from all the military advantages this entailed. By contrast the Free State army consisted of 8,000 men confined largely to the Dublin area and the midlands. Many of the Free State units stationed there were from other districts now under republican control and were unfamiliar with their new postings. But the Free State army held the advantage in terms of weaponry and British support.

By July 1922 the British government had supplied the Free State army with 11,900 rifles, 79 Lewis machine-guns, 4,200 revolvers, 3,500 hand grenades, armoured cars and artillery. If the war continued for any length of time the republicans would be forced to rely on weapons seizures for supplies, while the Free State army would be supplied regularly with as much weaponry as they needed by the British. In addition the Free State army enjoyed the full support of the British navy, who provided them with transportation, wireless communication, ammunition, searchlights and fuel. The British navy played a crucial role in deciding the outcome of the Irish Civil War by patrolling Irish waters and preventing IRA gunrunning. By August the British navy had three light cruisers, eleven destroyers, nine mine-sweepers and other auxiliary vessels stationed in Irish waters.[35]

The Free State army also had a financial advantage. The Bank of Ireland, which had initially been reluctant to respond to the Provisional Government's requests for £1 million in financial credit, reversed this decision in July and loosened its purse strings, quelling mutinous grumblings by some unpaid Free State soldiers. And, finally, the Free State had the support of the hierarchy of the Catholic Church in Ireland. The Catholic bishops had already demonstrated their pro-Treaty stance. They based their support on the argument that the majority of the people in Ireland would accept the Treaty, but undoubtedly the Church's stance played a very important part in shaping that acceptance. The same logic was not used by the Catholic Church during the War of Independence when the majority of people in Ireland supported the republic!

For these reasons the IRA needed to end the war with a quick and decisive victory over the Free State army. But they made the fatal mistake of retreating from Dublin as the fighting ended, leaving the capital under the control of the Free State government. This allowed the Free Staters to gain world-wide recognition as the lawful government in control of Ireland. However, the end of the fighting in Dublin, signalled the outbreak of civil war throughout the rest of the country.

CHAPTER 4

THE WAR COMES
TO LIMERICK

The fighting started in a haphazard fashion throughout the country as former friends and comrades who had been living in the vain hope that war could be avoided, now committed themselves to the battle. Despite its numerical superiority, the IRA's military capacity was very disorganised and had been further weakened when the republicans in the Four Courts surrendered, as a result of which three of the IRA's most capable leaders, Rory O'Connor, Liam Mellows and Tom Barry, had been captured. The IRA in the six counties was crushed between British, unionist and Free State forces and was unable to mount anything more than a token resistance to either the unionist or Free State governments in support of a united independent republic. In the Free

State-controlled areas of Dublin and Leinster, the IRA were unable to operate and most IRA men fled to republican-controlled areas. The remainder were re-organised by Ernie O'Malley, who had escaped from his Free State captors after the Four Courts surrender on 30 June and began mounting small scale sniping and guerrilla operations against the Free State army in Wicklow and Wexford.

Liam Lynch ordered all IRA volunteers to return to their command areas to prepare for all out war. Acting on Lynch's orders the IRA began consolidating their positions in the rest of Ireland and formed a strongly defended frontier stretching from Limerick city in a south-easterly direction all the way to Waterford.

Free State forces throughout the country were also preparing for war. When the fighting began in Dublin, Free State troops from Michael Brennan's 1st Western Division and Donncadh O'Hannigan's 4th Southern Division converged on Coolbawn House in Castleconnell, about six miles to the north-east of Limerick city. Brennan and O'Hannigan had between 700 and 800 troops under their command, but many were raw recruits who had not fought in the War of Independence. To add to Brennan's woes he was short of arms, having only 200 rifles with which to defend his divisional area, which included the whole of Clare and a large part of south-east Galway. O'Hannigan's division had a total of only 160 rifles. Determined to capture the city they marched unopposed towards the suburbs. Still lacking the military might to challenge the IRA troops in the city's barracks through direct attack, they entered the city by Clare Street and occupied the custom house, the courthouse, St Mary's cathedral, Mary Street police barracks and other buildings in the area around the Potato Market. These positions overlooked the Strand barracks on the northern shore of the Shannon and Thomond bridge, thereby isolating the IRA garrisons in the Strand and Castle barracks from their comrades in the Ordnance and New barracks to the south of the city. Free State troops rushed into Cruise's Hotel, which had until recently housed the Auxiliaries, and the houses on the opposite side of the street and immediately started digging a trench across the road to connect them. Racing across the empty streets and forcing in the doors of the buildings they came to, they advanced as far as Sarsfield bridge by breaking through the walls of each house until they reached the south side of the bridge. Here they threw a double barricade across the southern end of the bridge in an effort to hold back any IRA advance from the nearby Strand barracks.

Brennan established his headquarters in Cruise's Hotel and reinforced General Murphy's garrisons in the nearby William Street police barracks and in Limerick prison. A ring of buildings surrounding the hotel and the barracks was also commandeered by Brennan's troops including Cannock's and McBirney's houses in Denmark Street at the rear of the barracks, and Todd's shop on the opposite side of William Street. Next the Free State troops started building barricades across the entrances to O'Connell Street, William Street and Denmark Street. Within a short time Wickham Street, High Street and William Street Junction were also sealed off. With a defensive ring now drawn around his command post, Brennan stationed snipers in the windows of the buildings on these streets, which were mostly houses and shops. Brennan's men also established a direct line of supply or retreat east along the Dublin road into Clare along the Corbally road and the Ennis railway line. In a single swoop the Free State troops had captured key buildings in the heart of the city, dividing the IRA area of control into three, without a single shot being fired.

Brennan's main concern now, which he had mentioned in dispatches to Dublin, was lack of arms and ammunition. If the IRA discovered how poorly armed his troops were, they would mount an immediate attack and over-run his positions with little difficulty. Brennan gambled on a bluff to convince his opponents that he had the firepower to keep them at bay: 'Most of the men in these posts were unarmed but the few rifles they had were kept very much in evidence, and in some cases lengths of piping were used to simulate Lewis guns.'[36] His men who were lucky enough to be armed, peered nervously down the sights of their guns and awaited the republican response.

Despite his superior numbers, Liam Lynch failed to mount an immediate and direct attack on Brennan's positions, which could easily have forced them to retreat from Limerick city. However, the republicans in the rest of Munster were swift to respond to the outbreak of the Civil War. IRA units from Cork and Kerry quickly mobilised and began marching northwards through west Limerick towards the city. As they advanced they captured a number of Free State-held barracks and towns without much resistance, the exception being Foynes, where the barracks had to be set on fire before its Free State garrison would surrender. The republicans continued to advance unhindered as far as Adare, which the IRA captured from the Free State troops after a short battle, before they finally arrived to reinforce the garrison of local IRA volunteers stationed in the city's barracks in accordance with 10 March agreement.

Lynch had made one crucial mistake when the IRA occupied Limerick; although they controlled all of the main bridges in the city, he had not ordered any guard to be placed on Athlunkard bridge and the Free State troops had taken it without a challenge. Brennan realised the strategic value of this bridge and immediately began using it to bring Free State reinforcements into Limerick from his divisional headquarters in Ennis, thirty-five miles away. The unarmed Free State soldiers arrived by train in groups of fifty and disembarked at the Long Pavement railway station just across the river from Limerick. Here they were met by a lorry that had travelled from Brennan's headquarters laden with a rifle for each man. The newly armed reinforcements then marched in a group into the city, across Athlunkard bridge, to report to city headquarters – where they were promptly 'disarmed' and the same fifty rifles were immediately loaded onto another lorry and sent back to the Long Pavement to 'arm' the next group of reinforcements. This process was repeated several times each day. Lynch received updates as each group of seemingly well-armed and equipped reinforcements entered the city and was tricked into believing that Brennan's position was strengthening day by day. In fact Brennan had less than 150 rifles to arm the 400 troops he commanded in the city and only enough ammunition to last a day or two if fighting broke out against the 700 well-armed IRA volunteers commanded by Lynch.

Frank Aiken, commander of the 4th Northern Division of the IRA, who had so far adopted a neutral position, was friendly with both Lynch and Brennan, and with the help of Major Stephen O'Mara, Dan Breen and an Augustinian priest, arranged negotiations between the two in an attempt to prevent bloodshed. It was during these negotiations that Brennan realised his bluff had worked. Lynch based his proposals for an agreement with the Free State troops on the assumption that they commanded forces of equal strength. Had he known the real strength of Brennan's forces, Lynch could have contained them in Limerick city with only a quarter of his men and sent the rest to Dublin to strengthen the republican position there. So far Brennan had been lucky, and had entered talks with Lynch in the hope that more arms and reinforcements would arrive before his luck ran out:

> The whole Civil War really turned on Limerick … The
> Shannon was the barricade and whoever held Limerick held
> the whole south and the west.[37]

At this stage the south and west of the country was firmly
under republican control except for most of Clare, south
Galway, some areas in Longford, Roscommon and part of
Limerick county. According to Brennan:

> The importance of Limerick in this setup was painfully clear. The
> whole of Connacht and Munster became a solid block against
> the Treaty forces and Lynch was free to rush strong bodies of
> men to intervene in the Dublin fighting. At the worst, this could
> have involved the defeat of the Provisional Government; at best
> it would mean prolonged fighting in and around Dublin, then
> a fight through Connacht and Munster …, My whole fright
> was that Lynch would attack me before the guns turned up,
> because we couldn't last. I had to keep him talking to keep him
> from attacking. We met altogether about a dozen times. We
> used to meet in the presbytery of the Augustinian church where
> we argued and argued … If Lynch had attacked us we were
> helpless. He had plenty of lorries and could have been in Dublin
> in a matter of hours.[38]

The outcome of these discussions was a series of agreements
that neither side would attack the other. Their main aim was
to ensure that counties Limerick and Clare would stay out

of the Civil War. On 4 July, Donncadh O'Hannigan signed a formal truce on behalf of Brennan and the Free State garrison in Limerick:

6.30 p.m. 4/7/22

Agreement as between Comdt General O'Hannigan and C/S executive forces.

Agreed:

1. Commandant General O'Hannigan will not at any time attack executive forces; executive forces will not attack Commandant General O'Hannigan's forces.
2. The executive forces will not occupy any post in East Limerick Brigade area.
3. That both sides only occupy their normal number of posts in Limerick city and east Limerick.
4. That there will be no movement of armed troops in Limerick or East Limerick Brigade area, except by liaison agreement.
5. That Commandant General O'Hannigan withdraws any of his troops drafted into Limerick city since Saturday.
6. Executive communications to be maintained between 1st, 2nd & 3rd Southern divisional headquarters and Limerick city.
7. This agreement to hold during the period of fighting between executive forces and Beggars Bush or until both sides of the army find a solution to the problem.
8. We agree to these conditions in the practicable certainty

that national peace and unity will eventuate from our efforts and we guarantee to use every means in our power to get this peace.

9. This agreement to be put into effect by 12 o'clock tonight.[39]

Convinced that he had now neutralised Brennan and the 1st Western Division of the Free State army, Lynch believed that he had secured the whole south and west for the republic and was confident that the ongoing fight in Dublin would end in a republican victory. Immediately after O'Hannigan signed the truce, Lynch wrote to Ernie O'Malley in ecstatic mood: 'Limerick agreement means O'Hannigan and Brennan divisions are adopting a neutral attitude. This is glorious if they stand by their signatories.'[40] Lynch was wrong on all these counts. Dan Breen felt that Lynch was too much of an idealist and not the cold hard military pragmatist that the situation demanded:

He was an absolute dreamer and an idealist. He wasn't a man for the world. A monastery was his place ... He didn't understand compromise.[41]

It was not long before news of the agreement in Limerick reached Free State headquarters in Dublin. Eoin O'Duffy fully understood the strategic importance of the city and stressed to the Free State authorities: 'We cannot afford a defeat in Limerick as we might have to fight the whole 1st Southern

IRA Chief-of-Staff Liam Lynch, commander of the IRA forces in Limerick, July 1922.

Ernie O'Malley, commander of the IRA forces in Limerick, March 1922.

General Michael Brennan, commander of the 1st Western Division of the Free State army.

General Donncadh O'Hannigan, commander of the 4th Southern Division of the Free State army.

IRA volunteers arrive to reinforce republican positions in Limerick, March–April 1922. *Courtesy of Limerick Civic Museum*

IRA volunteer George Gunn, 1st Cork Brigade Active Service Unit, who was stationed in Russell's Mills during the fighting in Limerick city. *Courtesy of his son, Pat Gunn, Cork*

IRA garrison, Strand barracks, Limerick city. Their commander
Connie McNamara is seated on the far right.
Courtesy of Jim Corbett

Connie
McNamara
(left) and IRA
leaders after
taking over
the Ordnance
barracks,
Limerick city,
from British
troops.
*Courtesy of Jim
Corbett*

Free State troops occupying Cruise's Hotel.
Courtesy of Martin and Norma Naughton, Castleconnell

Free State
troops defend
a barricade
outside Cruise's
Hotel as the
fighting begins
in July 1922.
*Courtesy of
Limerick Civic
Museum*

Free State barricade on the streets of Limerick city.
Courtesy of Martin and Norma Naughton, Castleconnell

Free State soldiers inspect the damage at the main door of the Strand barracks after shelling and surrender.
Courtesy of Limerick Civic Museum

After a long, bitter fight, Free State troops celebrate the surrender by IRA forces of the Strand barracks by posing for a photograph at a breach in the back wall caused by Free State shelling.
Courtesy of Limerick Civic Museum

Civilians looting the Ordnance barracks after its burning by the
retreating IRA forces.
Courtesy of Martin and Norma Naughton, Castleconnell

The burning of the New barracks by retreating IRA forces.
Courtesy of Limerick Civic Museum

Free State soldiers arrive to inspect the ruins of the New barracks.
Courtesy of Limerick Civic Museum

The victors. General Eoin O'Duffy (left), General William Murphy
(centre) and General Michael Brennan (right) in Limerick city
after the republican withdrawal.
Courtesy of the National Library of Ireland

WHO ARE THE

CRIMINALS NOW

Capt. Danford, I.R.A. lies dead in his home, his body **riddled by bullets supplied by L. George** to his new Imperial Forces—for the destruction of the Republicans who cannot **conscientiously give allegiance to England's King.**

His young wife and five infant orphans bemoan the loss of their protector and provider---so that the British Empire may flourish and keep its hold on Ireland.

On Monday night, this brave Soldier, who fought for the Republic during all the terrors of the Black and Tans, was arrested in a relatives house in Roxboro by Capt. Quin, late of the British Army and Messrs. Gilligan and Walsh all of the Free State Army.

His dead body was removed from the brick works at Clino on the following morning in a Red Cross car, to his home.

No other facts have as yet transpired.

A few weeks ago Lieut. Hogan, Denis O'Dwyer and a lad named O'Farrell were arrested near Rathkeale by Free State soldiers.

AFTER ARREST, they were fired on by their captors, Denis O'Dwyer being instantly killed and the others wounded.

Lieut. Hogan later died of wounds in St. John's Hospital, but a few days before his death, he made a sworn deposition before the Deputy Mayor Mr. Paul O'Brien and Mr. M. Doyle, both Republican Magistrates

This statement has been suppressed.

Both those murdered prisoners were laid to the last rest without even the pretence of an inquest.

We demand the publication of this dying statement immediately, we also demand of the Chief Acting Magistrate of the City that **a full and sworn public inquiry** be held into this **latest and most Cowardly Murder.**

'Who are the Criminals now'.
Republican propaganda leaflet about Free State killings in the city
after the battle for Limerick.
Courtesy of Des Long

[Division of the IRA] in Limerick.'[42] As soon as rumours reached O'Duffy at Free State army GHQ in Dublin, that Brennan and O'Hannigan were negotiating a settlement with Lynch, he dispatched General Dermot McManus to Limerick to assess and take control of the situation.

Acting on O'Duffy's orders McManus set out for Limerick through hostile territory disguised as a tramp and arrived in Limerick on 5 July. On arrival he immediately informed Lynch that he had orders to commence military action against the IRA and cancel O'Hannigan's agreement. He also declared that neither O'Hannigan nor Brennan had had the authority to make such an agreement on behalf of the Free State army:

To: Liam Lynch, Chief of Staff, Executive Forces, New Barracks, Limerick.

A Chara,

This is to inform you that I arrived here from Dublin this evening with definite instructions from GHQ as to military operations in this area. Before coming into this area I made arrangements for certain positions to be taken up immediately. On arriving at Cruise's Hotel, I discovered that Commandant General Brennan, and Commandant General O'Hannigan, had been discussing terms of agreement with you for some days past.

I have definite instructions that no such agreement even if signed could be admitted by GHQ and these officers had no authority whatever to enter into such agreement.

I hear that another meeting between these officers and yourself has been arranged for 8 a.m. today. I have instructed them that this meeting is not to take place and that they are to have no further communication with you on this matter. I herewith reserve full liberty of action, and I have made certain dispositions to protect my posts in the city and their communications.

Signed D.A. Mac Maghunusa[43]

McManus was alarmed at the situation and was concerned about the loyalty of Brennan and his troops:

I found the morale of the Divisional Staff extremely low. All ideas were centred on (a) How best an attack by the enemy could be postponed or avoided by compromise and agreement and, (b) How long we could … hold out when besieged.[44]

He reported to Free State army headquarters:

Unless rifles and armoured cars arrive within 24 hours of now, 10 a.m. 6/7/22, we will be in very grave danger of disaster … I feel confident that I can finish off and capture the whole of the executive [executive forces, IRA] in this area in a few days. There is, however, this real danger. Comdt-Gen. Brennan is seriously anxious for a truce and an agreement. He may come to an understanding with Lynch and when I repudiate it, resign, and probably a large part of his division with him.[45]

Poor communications, and failure to realise just how desperate Brennan's situation in Limerick was, meant that those in Free State headquarters were suspicious of Brennan's motives, loyalties and willingness to negotiate. Brennan was in an impossible situation. Free State army headquarters would not send him the guns he needed to fight and this had forced him to negotiate with Lynch; and because he had negotiated with Lynch they would not send him the guns to fight. In the meantime Brennan assembled the senior officers under his command and explained the situation to them. They agreed with his strategy and to further stall Lynch by signing another truce agreement. Lynch signed this agreement despite McManus' letter, as he believed that Brennan's troops would remain loyal to their commander and follow his orders. The signing took place on 7 July:

AGREEMENT

We agree, in the interests of a united Ireland, and to save our country from utter destruction, to call a meeting of Divisional Commandants representing the First and Second Southern Divisions, and the First Western Division of the Executive forces, Irish Republican Army, and the Divisional Commandants representing the Fourth Southern Division and Mid Western Division and the Mid Western Command of the Dáil [Provisional Government] forces, Irish Republican Army [Free State]. The meeting to be held as soon as Séan MacEoin can be got into this area. The conference to be held in Limerick.

The forces now opposed to one another in Limerick city end for all time this fratricidal strife in view of the meeting of the Divisional Commandants in Limerick. And as a guarantee of good faith towards a permanent agreement the Divisional Council of the Fourth Southern Division and Mid Western Division and the Mid Western Command of the Dáil Forces, IRA, agree to hand in their resignations if agreement is not reached at the meeting of Divisional Commandants. The agreement as regards the resignations of the Divisional Commandants to be signed by Saturday evening. The buildings to be occupied by the Dáil forces, Irish Republican Army are the Custom House, the Jail, the Courthouse, Cruise's Hotel and William Street police barracks. The troops of the Executive forces, Irish Republican Army [will] be withdrawn to barracks. No troops in Limerick city to appear in public with arms except by liaison agreement. A truce now exists between Executive forces IRA and First Western Division and Fourth Southern Division Dáil forces, Irish Republican Army until the conference ends between the Divisional Commandants. All outposts to be withdrawn to the agreed centres by 6 o'clock Friday evening, 7 July 1922. This agreement takes effect from the moment it is signed – 1.30 a.m. 7 July 1922.

Liam Lynch, C.S. Executive Forces, IRA
Donncadh O'Hannigan, Comdt-General 4th Southern Division
M. Brennan, Commandt Gen. 1st Western Division.[46]

This agreement was witnessed by Father Hennessy, OSM, and the Mayor of Limerick, Stephen O'Mara.

With the fall of Dublin to the Free State army, all eyes were now focused upon the city of Limerick. McManus, who had been inspecting Free State army units in Clare, returned to Limerick on 7 July and having assessed the situation wrote to Lynch that he was 'willing to allow this matter [the truce between Lynch and Brennan] to go ahead on condition that there is no change in the military position here.'[47] Allowing the unsteady truce to remain, McManus made his way back to Dublin to report to Collins and the leaders of the Free State army, who decided that O'Duffy would march on Limerick and take over command of the south-west from Brennan.

Lynch was still hoping for victory without further bloodshed. According to Paddy Coughlin, an IRA volunteer from Mitchelstown in Cork, 'Liam Lynch did not want a war'. Lynch also hoped that his actions would take the three Free State military commanders involved in the negotiations Brennan, O'Hannigan and Seán MacEoin – out of the fighting. After the 7 July agreement was signed he wrote: 'I expect we will control from Shannon to Carlow in a day or two', and claimed that the agreement gave the IRA:

… a very considerable military advantage, as with a comparably small number of troops held up in Limerick, we have been able to ensure that at least 3,000 FS troops are also held up. Had we to fight in Limerick, our forces that are in Limerick would not only be held up for ten days, but we wouldn't be in a position to reinforce Wexford-New Ross area nor could we hope to attack Thurles. The most we could do would be to harass Kilkenny.[48]

However, the IRA Director of Operations, Seán Moylan, disagreed with Lynch's policy and called on Liam Deasy to send more IRA volunteers from the 1st Southern Division to Limerick to prepare for an attack on the Free State army there:

To O/C 1st Southern Division,

1. I must get one hundred riflemen, ten machine-guns and gun crews sent on from Cork 1 and Kerry at once. The Staters are in force – well equipped and I must hold the offensive ...

2. Cork 1 can send a bunch of right good men, so can Kerry. Let us have them. There is no use in fooling around with this question any longer. Send on the men and let us get on with the war. Hope the Lads are O.K. What about sending a few hundred grenades?

Seán Moylan

[P.S.] Could Cork 3 send us fifty men? S.M.[49]

Seán Hyde, commander of the IRA's Western Command, protested to Liam Deasy, Adjutant of the IRA's 1st Southern Division: 'This is a game of ping pong. If we don't take them on today we'll have to take them on tomorrow.'[50]

But even if it wouldn't deliver a long term military victory, the agreement gave Lynch a short term propaganda victory. He immediately published the content of the agreement. The Free State army command was already concerned about Michael Brennan's loyalty and commitment, and the publication of the details of the second truce played on Free States fears that the agreement might lead to Brennan's whole command in the 1st Western Division either refusing to fight or defecting en masse to the republican side. However, regardless of the agreement, the commanders of the Free State army were determined to capture Limerick and had already dispatched Free State troops fresh from the fighting in Dublin, under the command of Commandant Seamus Hogan, with the arms and ammunition Brennan so desperately needed to capture the city: 150 Free State troops, armour-plated lorries and armoured cars.

Two lorry-loads of Brennan's troops from Ennis were travelling north to reach Hogan's column and help guide it to Limerick when they were ambushed by the IRA on the Gort road. The first Free State lorry managed to force its way through the ambush position, but the second turned back towards their temporary barracks at the courthouse in Ennis where they came under attack again from republican snipers.

On their journey south from Galway the soldiers travelling in Hogan's column met stern resistance from the IRA in the area around Gort. Private Michael Lawless was one of them:

I joined the regular National Army in Beggars Bush after the Treaty and worked for a while there, at chemicals under Commandant Dan Stapleton. On the outbreak of the Civil War I was in the armoured car 'Sliabh na mBan' and was at the capture of the Gresham. I was in the armoured car after firing had ceased when a final shot from somewhere wounded Dan Stapleton. Shortly afterwards, in July '22 probably, I was sent in a convoy to Limerick under Comdt James Hogan. We went via Athlone and at Kilchreest, Co. Galway were ambushed and I was nearly killed. A soldier called Charley [sic] O'Connor was killed.[51]

Private Gerry O'Connor of the Free State army was killed at Kilchreest near Gort on 8 July 1922. He was a native of Victoria Street, Dublin and was married with three children.

Despite these difficulties Hogan's convoy arrived in Scarriff, in east Clare on the morning of 11 July. The journey from Dublin had taken three days due to the heavy weight of the vehicles on poor roads and IRA activity in the midlands and on the Clare–Galway border. Hogan sent word to Brennan to collect the arms on the morning of 11 July. Hogan had been briefed by O'Duffy to use the opportunity to assess Brennan's loyalty to the Free State, and had been instructed that if he was not satisfied to push on south towards Limerick and try to take the city himself without Brennan's help. Hogan, who knew Brennan from the War of Independence, was satisfied with his explanation of the difficulties he faced and why he had entered into negotiations with Lynch. He handed over the weapons and armoured vehicles to Brennan's command.

Now that he had reinforcements and the firepower to assert the Free State's authority in Limerick, Brennan no longer needed to keep bluffing Lynch. On his journey back to Limerick, Brennan received the news that a Free State soldier had been shot and killed during an altercation with an IRA unit and used this pretext to send a message to Lynch on his return to Limerick, breaking the truce. Privates Michael O'Connell and Thomas O'Brien, stationed at William Street police barracks, had been ordered to go to Nelson Street to commandeer cars, furniture and any other material they could to build barricades. O'Connell was surprised by IRA volunteers at Roches Street corner, disarmed and arrested. O'Brien, who was following close behind, apparently offered resistance when confronted by the republicans and was shot dead. Now there was no turning back.

Two hours later, the Free State troops in William Street opened fire on the IRA garrison in the Ordnance barracks. By now Brennan's troops were on the move, commandeering buildings in the city centre and erecting new barricades and street defences. Low intensity fighting broke out between the Free State army and the IRA, as both sides continued to erect makeshift barricades. Seán Hyde sent an immediate dispatch to Liam Deasy appealing for reinforcements:

To O/C 1st Southern,

1. The situation has got very serious here during the last hour or so. FS troops have swarmed into the city like bees and occupied practically all the posts we held last week.

2. Already casualties have been reported among our men who were raising barricades.

3. The enemy have a plentiful supply of armoured cars and steel-plated lorries.

4. Firing occurs only at long intervals & no machine-guns have been used so far.

5. Help no matter how small would be welcome.

6. Great care should be observed from Adare to City, and better communicate with us before rushing any troops in here to barracks.

7. Find dispatches for SHQ.

S. Hyde.[52]

As soon as Lynch was informed about what had happened, he realised that the Free State army was on the brink of a major victory which would change the whole nature of the war. He wrote to Ernie O'Malley: 'The second agreement reached at Limerick has been broken by the enemy ... I believe ... we will eventually have to destroy all our posts and have to operate as of old in columns.'[53]

CHAPTER 5

THE BATTLE FOR LIMERICK

TUESDAY EVENING, 11 JULY

The fighting in the city began in Upper William Street with a Free State attack on the Ordnance barracks and quickly spread through the centre of the city to Lower William Street, Roches Street and Thomas Street. The crack of rifle fire, the dull thud of grenades exploding in distant streets and wild rumours soon spread news of the outbreak of hostilities to the ears of the garrisons in more far flung posts. Some combatants, like Connie Neenan, leader of the IRA's 1st Cork Brigade, received no official notice of the ending of the ceasefire agreement. He was returning to the city from Ballyneety by car and only discovered that a fight had begun when he arrived in the battle zone:

The people in charge on the spot were [Dan 'Sandow'] Donovan, Mick Murphy and myself. The Staters that were there were far better organised and in greater numbers. They had seized posts and we had seized posts. We had occupied as far as William Street, but firing had not commenced at this stage. They had, however, taken some prisoners at Ballyneety four miles outside [Limerick city]. I was deputised with a local volunteer to meet their commandant, Tommy Murphy, to seek the release of these prisoners ... When I returned to Limerick I found that fighting had started. They had started it. I was a lucky man that I had not been taken prisoner.[54]

The IRA was concentrated mostly in the Upper O'Connell Street area and the docks on the south-eastern bank of the Shannon. The Free State army held a pocket of territory in the area east of Lower William Street around Denmark Street, Ellen Street and Patrick Street. Beyond this, the city's districts were a confused mixture of republican and Free State outposts, with neither side in complete control of any of the surrounding streets and many of the areas in between frequently changing hands in sniping battles, attacks and counter-attacks. The north-western bank of the Shannon was dominated from the Strand barracks by the republicans under the command of Captain Cornelius McNamara (known by his men as Connie Mackey) and IRA snipers on the western side of Thomond bridge near the Treaty Stone. However, their control of this side of the Shannon was challenged by Free State soldiers concentrated in the Union Workhouse (now St Camillus' hospital) and Strand Cottage, a large private house near the Condensed Milk factory (at the western side of the New bridge today). Furthermore, small bodies of Free State soldiers from Michael Brennan's 1st Western Division in east Clare had been mobilised and a steady trickle were arriving to join the attack on the IRA at Strand barracks with every passing hour.

Directly east of the river on King's Island, an IRA garrison under the command of Stephen Kennedy held the Castle barracks and the area at the eastern end of Thomond bridge, but the Castle was surrounded by Free State soldiers stationed in private houses. The Free State army also controlled the courthouse, the women's prison, the Potato Market and the custom house. The republicans had control of most of the eastern approaches to the city on the Tipperary road, occupying St Joseph's asylum, and further in towards the city centre they had control of most of Upper William Street from the Ordnance barracks and Shaw's Bacon Factory. However, their occupation of this area was interrupted by the small force of Free State troops that held Limerick prison and the Munster Fair Tavern next to Mount Saint Lawrence Cemetery, and the Free State army launched frequent attacks on the republican barricades and outposts surrounding the Ordnance barracks from Lower William Street and Lower Gerald Griffin Street. To the south the IRA held the areas of Raheen and Ballinacurra and was able to rush in republican reinforcements as far as the New barracks from North Cork, Charleville and Buttevant, and in County Limerick as soon as the fighting started.

With the outbreak of fighting in Limerick, the city's workers were unable to go to their employment in the city's factories and shops without fear of being shot in the crossfire and so all trade and commerce ground to a halt. Tony McMahon, a young boy in Limerick at the time, describes the scene:

> The area around St Joseph Street, Edward Street, Bowman Street and Wolfe Tone Street was a veritable no man's land; pinned in between the New barracks and a Free State sniper on the tower of St Michael's church, Barrington Street, the people were unable to get out to buy food and provisions. The troops in the New barracks set up a food depot in St Ita's School in St Joseph Street. Men and women normally working in the grocery and provision trade were selected to prepare and parcel food for each day's ration to the families. The bulk of the foodstuffs, flour, sugar, bacon and tea, were brought to the depot each morning by the troops. There was enough for everyone and there were no complaints.
>
> The forces in the New barracks had a prisoner who came from St Joseph Street. He had an IRA record but took the Treaty side, so his erstwhile comrades detained him in the barracks. His younger brother and a school pal were sent to the barracks with clothes for the prisoner. They went again on the next day but the barrack officials became suspicious and kept them in custody.[55]

The Free State sniper on St Michael's church tower had a perfect aim and he inflicted many injuries on the republican troops as they moved around the barrack square. To obstruct his view, a rope was stretched across the square and blankets dropped from it. But the sniper was not long in picking off the rope and the drapes collapsed leaving the square exposed to his rifle again.

By nightfall neither side had gained any substantial advantage in the fighting. The men on both sides snatched what few minutes or hours of sleep they could while sentries stood watch, only to be woken from their slumber by the occasional rattle of a machine-gun or nearby rifle fire when those on duty, ever fearful of imminent attack, saw some distant movement in the shadows of the summer night. Before returning to his native Cork to organise reinforcement and supplies for the republicans in Limerick, Liam Deasy consulted with Liam Lynch late that night:

I visited Lynch and Donovan in New barracks, Limerick. They gave me a complete picture of the situation but with Liam's optimism, and this was something which ruled his life to the end, he felt that we could drive the Free State troops from the city. In my heart of hearts I could not see this being accomplished, and many old friends to whom I spoke while I was there felt the same and had no great enthusiasm to meet former comrades in actual battle. I returned to Mallow with a heavy heart …[56]

WEDNESDAY 12 JULY

On the following morning, fully confident of a republican victory in Limerick city, Liam Lynch moved his headquarters to Clonmel in County Tipperary. His spirits and his belief in an ultimate victory for the Republic had been boosted by the news that on their way to Limerick as reinforcements, IRA volunteers from Cork had captured Caherconlish barracks from the Free State army earlier that morning. They had taken Richard O'Connell, commander of the Free State army in the Mid Limerick Brigade area, William Hayes, leader of the Free State army in East Limerick, and five other Free State officers prisoner, including Joe Graham and John Joe O'Brien.

Hayes, Graham and O'Brien were taken to Pallasgreen on the Limerick–Tipperary border by the IRA. While they were held captive here an altercation took place between William Hayes and a red-haired IRA volunteer who Hayes accused of having been an informer for the British during the War of Independence. The tension increased further when Seán Hogan, a member of the IRA who had been rescued from British custody at Knocklong railway station on 13 May 1919 by an IRA party that included John Joe O'Brien, deliberately snubbed O'Brien by pretending not to recognise him. O'Brien snapped that if he had realised Hogan would become such a lowlife, he would never have risked his life to save him.[57]

On Wednesday morning, fierce fighting broke out in the docklands area along Henry Street, Cecil Street, Steam Boat Quay and Bishops Quay as Free State troops launched a sweeping attack from the centre of the city towards the river. In this area the IRA were lodged in Russell's Mills, the GPO, Daly's Bakery and buildings on the docks.

On Sarsfield Street, Free State soldiers had taken up position in houses on one side, from where they fired on the bread delivery vans and their armed IRA guards emerging from Daly's Bakery. These vans were attempting to deliver bread to the IRA positions and civilian food depots. The Free State troops also mounted sniping attacks on the bakery itself, isolating the republicans and trapping them inside. The men in the bakery had been supplied with food from the New barracks up to this point, but during the Free State's four-day attack they had nothing to eat but bread.

Free State troops also began advancing through Bedford Row and along O'Connell Street south-westwards in an attempt to reach the docks. IRA volunteers inside the GPO on Lower Cecil Street came under attack from Free State soldiers advancing from the Roches Street area and suffered their first casualty when an IRA volunteer in the nearby telephone exchange was shot dead by a sniper's bullet. However, the republicans managed to repel the Free State attack on the GPO, forcing them to retreat. One Free State soldier was badly wounded in Roches Street and Sergeant Patrick Stapleton of the Free State army was killed as he directed his men in an attack on the republicans from the water tank on the roof of Boyd's shop.

On O'Connell Street the republicans tunnelled from one building to the next through the rooms on the first floor of each building and were able to secure control of a stretch of the street from the National Bank to Messrs Nash and Sons. A row of houses on the opposite side of the street beside the Provincial Bank was also linked up in the same way. Only seven civilians – Mr McNamara, manager of the National Bank, his wife and daughter, a Mrs Hayes, her daughter and her friend and Mr Moloney, a chemist who owned a business on O'Connell Street – were permitted to remain in this area during the fighting and only because they were adamant about staying. However, the *Clare Champion* reported that, even in the thick of the fighting, people living locally were permitted to call at Moloney's Chemist for supplies:

> All speak well of the dozen Irregulars [IRA] who constituted the garrison, and it was not an uncommon thing for a person in need of infant's food or such like, stocked by Mr Moloney, chemist, in the middle of the block, to call at the bank and secure what was required in a very short space of time.[58]

In a different part of the city a Free State attack took place on the Ordnance barracks in Upper William Street, during which Michael Moynihan from Sandmall in Limerick city, a member of Na Fianna Éireann, was shot. Moynihan had been acting as a messenger for the garrison and was looking out one of the barracks' windows when he was shot in the stomach by a Free State sniper. IRA volunteer Joe Nash rushed to Moynihan's aid and put pressure on the wound to slow the bleeding, but he knew that it was useless. As Nash pressed down on Moynihan's wound he caught the wounded boy's gaze and could 'see the life draining from him'.[59] A group of republicans rushed the boy to Saint John's hospital, but he was pronounced dead upon arrival. The *Clare Champion*'s correspondent reported from Limerick on Saturday 15 July: 'Sniping is intermittent. There is a halt at times. Then suddenly the calm of the city is disturbed by the rattle of machine-gun and rifle fire, which continues for some hours.'

During the day, Free State troops continued to attempt to reinforce their forces within the city. That evening, at 7.30 p.m., three car-loads of Free State soldiers advancing on Limerick ran into a republican road block at Patrickswell, in County Limerick. After a quick running battle, the Free State soldiers retreated through the fields on the roadside, having abandoned their cars, some explosives, a number of prepared mines and some guns to the republicans.

THURSDAY 13 JULY

During the third day of fighting in Limerick, Liam Lynch issued a propaganda bulletin from his new headquarters in

Clonmel in an attempt to boost the morale of republican forces in Limerick:

Official Bulletin

2nd Southern Division.

The agreement reached in Limerick city which covered Limerick city and east Limerick Brigade areas has now been broken by the Free State officers who signed it. Fighting is in progress at the moment there.

GHQ is in close touch with the O/C operations there and reports to hand show that our lines of communication are working splendidly. Our troops hold the initiative now. One enemy sniper was picked off the parapet of the Catholic Institute near William Street. A republican boy scout was killed near Ordnance barracks. One of our men killed in telephone exchange by enemy sniper.

Reinforcements reached New barracks from Cork district. Reinforcements moving to Limerick captured a party of enemy. Rifles, mines etc. and five enemy motor cars were captured by our troops in this engagement.

Telephonic communication with Limerick completely cut. Heavy fighting reported: Ordnance and in Co. Clare district at rear of Strand barracks. Fighting developing gradually along front from Ordnance barracks to Newtonperrie [Russell's] Mills. A sharp engagement in Thomas Street. Three enemy killed and four or five wounded. No casualties on our side. Not less than six men have left Free State forces and are now fighting with us.[60]

But despite the IRA's successes in capturing the Free State-held barracks at Caherconlish in County Limerick and stopping the Free State reinforcements from reaching Limerick at Patrickswell, more Free State forces were already closing in on the city through south Galway, east Clare and Tipperary to join in the fight.

Private John Pinkman of the Free State army was on his way towards the city from Dublin, through the midlands and Tipperary, with a Free State army motorised column under the command of Tom Flood. Born in Liverpool of Irish parents he had joined the IRA at the age of sixteen and was imprisoned in Dartmoor prison during the War of Independence. He was released after the Truce in 1921 and had travelled to Ireland to join the 'Dublin Guards' unit of the Free State army:

When attempts begun on Tuesday 11 July failed to dislodge the Irregulars from their positions in Limerick city, our GHQ announced on 13 July the appointment of General Eoin O'Duffy as O/C South Western Command, and ordered additional troops into the drive against the Irregular forces in that area. Our flying column was to spearhead that drive, and to strengthen and support the bulk of the force which consisted largely of raw, inexperienced soldiers ... The numerical strength of the Irregulars – on paper at least – was greater than ours and they had seized large quantities of arms and ammunition from those barracks vacated by the departing troops. They had, with the acquiescence of the British, confiscated the cargo of military supplies aboard the British Admiralty vessel the *Upnor* at the end of March ... We arrived at Nenagh tired and hungry about nine o'clock in the evening, and after a good meal we bunked down for the night in the old British army barracks while the regular garrison stood guard.[61]

With reinforcements approaching from the north, Michael Brennan and William Murphy were attempting to use the superior military hardware the Free State army had been given by the British government to turn the tide of the fighting in their favour.

On Thursday morning the IRA mounted an attack on the Munster Fair Tavern and captured it. However, they were only to hold this position for a few hours. During the afternoon, using armoured cars Free State forces dashed up Lane Street breaking through a number of republican barricades and took the Munster Fair Tavern, capturing fourteen prisoners. The Free State armoured car, 'Danny Boy', had arrived in Limerick city with Seamus Hogan's column late on the evening of 11 July. The vehicle came into the city from the Dublin road and managed to make it to Free State headquarters in William Street police barracks. The day after it arrived, the IRA used a mine to blow up Annacotty bridge over the River Mulcair to prevent further armoured vehicles or troop transports reaching William Street by this route. Upper William Street was heavily barricaded and mined by the IRA garrison, stretching from the Ordnance barracks all the way up to the Munster Fair Tavern at the corner of Mount Saint Lawrence Cemetery. The only Free State post in this stretch of territory was Limerick prison. 'Danny Boy' attempted to break through the republican barricades with the intention of mounting a direct attack on the Ordnance barracks. The Free State army had used the armoured car in the previous two days to spearhead its attack. Knowing that the IRA had mined the street and the approach to the prison, on Tuesday and Wednesday the car had approached the barricades and raced towards them stopping, starting, advancing and retreating at different speeds in an attempt to make the republicans panic and detonate their mines prematurely. Each time it halted, the armoured car and the Free State soldiers, advancing from a relatively safe distance behind, opened fire on the IRA volunteers inside the Ordnance barracks raking the windows and outer walls of the building with machine-gun and rifle fire.

Having failed in several attempts to break through the republican barricades, 'Danny Boy' moved to the other end of the republican-held territory via Mulgrave Street and Lane Street, halting a few feet from the front of the Munster Fair Tavern. 'Danny Boy' opened fire on the IRA men inside with its Vickers machine-gun. Although the republicans put up the best resistance they could, their rifle fire was useless against an armoured vehicle. After five minutes resistance under intense machine-gun fire from the armoured car, the Free State troops called on the fourteen IRA volunteers inside to surrender. They were warned that if they did not comply hand grenades would be thrown through the shattered windows. After a few moments the men inside the Munster Fair Tavern threw out their arms and were taken prisoner. They were marched up the street to Limerick prison, becoming its first republican prisoners. The Free State troops immediately returned to the tavern and reinforced it, erecting new barricades to prevent the approach of any more IRA units from east Limerick and Tipperary advancing towards the city. Now the Free Staters controlled most of the city's perimeter, with only the suburbs in Ballinacurra and Raheen remaining under republican command.

Not to be outdone by the Free State army's superior technology, the men of the IRA's 1st Cork Brigade stationed in the New barracks had managed to create their own make-shift armoured car by building steel plates and scrap metal onto the body of a lorry. It was fitted with heavy iron wheels with solid rubber tyres and had two revolving turrets both equipped with Hotchkiss machine-guns. The IRA volunteers who built it christened it 'The Hooded Terror', and it would see its first action on Thursday evening.

At 5 p.m. that evening the IRA units based in the docklands area on the south-west of the River Shannon attempted to advance from the GPO on Lower Cecil Street through to the Free State army headquarters in William

Street. Their attack failed, but not before they had wounded two Free State snipers on top of Cleeve's building and dislodged another from his perch in Woolworth's stores, forcing him to retreat to the County Club.

At 9.15 p.m. Cork No. 1 Brigade, accompanied by their armoured car, advanced to Roches Corner from the New barracks and after a seven-minute firefight established a post there and a second outpost on the opposite side of the street. Fifteen minutes later, the republicans attempted a further advance. In response, a double turret Free State armoured car and three armoured lorries were rushed to the scene from William Street. A fierce battle erupted with the Free State soldiers opening up an attack on the new IRA positions using the armoured vehicles, machine-guns and rifle grenades. The Free State counter-attack proved unsuccessful and they were forced to retreat leaving the IRA in command of Roches Corner.

The final combat on Thursday took place outside the city. At midnight the IRA units in County Limerick surrounded and captured Kilmallock barracks from the Free State army, after a determined attack forced the defenders to surrender.

With the battle for Limerick intensifying and the casualties multiplying on both sides, the plight of the city's civilian population was now becoming desperate and under the cover of darkness over 300 people from the streets which had borne the brunt of the fighting, fled to the countryside:

Many families from the 'No Mans Land' area left their homes and started a trek to Mungret College, then vacant during the summer holidays. The Jesuit fathers generously opened their doors, and food and shelter were given to hundreds of women and children. The men who had accompanied them to the college, when they were satisfied that their families were safe, proceeded to Cooperhill Farm, Ballybrown. The owners of the farm were also generous in their hospitality and were highly spoken of afterwards.[62]

FRIDAY 14 JULY

On the morning of the fourth day of the battle, the Free State army stormed Daly's Bakery and captured the IRA garrison inside without casualties. The way was now clear for a scouting patrol from the bakery to move towards the docks and it was sent along Henry Street in the direction of the republican barricades at Russell's Mills. The scouts came under heavy fire from the mill and fell back with three wounded. Thirty Free State troops, including a Lewis gunner, then began an advance along Henry Street. They were followed at a distance by two groups of twenty soldiers in a slow cautious movement designed to test the enemy's firepower by advancing slowly, pausing and advancing a little further before pausing again. Eventually the Free State soldiers set up their Lewis gun in a third storey window on Henry Street and, with the advantage of height, were able to rake the republican barricades and Russell's Mills with machine-gun fire.

Now under sustained machine-gun and rifle fire, and without any sign of reinforcements coming from the New barracks, the IRA volunteers inside the mill had two options open to them. They could try to defend the building alone, with few supplies and little chance of success, or they could attempt to break through the lines of advancing Free State soldiers and fight their way to their comrades in the Glentworth Hotel. With the Free State soldiers gaining ground they opted for the latter. IRA volunteer George Gunn, from the 1st Cork Brigade Active Service Unit, was evacuating the mill with another republican when they were fired on by the Free State soldiers as they made a frantic dash across Henry Street. Gunn's comrade lost his hat as he ran and instinctively paused for a split second, turning mid-stride to retrieve it. He was instantly killed by a burst of machine-gun fire from the Lewis gun mounted in Henry Street, much to the horror of Gunn who had managed to reach the other side alive.[63]

The IRA's evacuation of the mill and the accuracy of the Free State troop's machine-gun gave the Free State control of this area and the scouting patrol now managed to reach the GPO. After a bloody struggle during which the building changed hands three times, the IRA volunteers inside were forced into a fighting retreat and the building was finally taken by the Free State attackers, along with the telephone exchange near the GPO.

The IRA had been using the telephone exchange to relay news of the fighting in Limerick to Lynch's command in Clonmel. They had also been able to intercept phone calls between the different Free State posts and learn about troop movements. When the building was about to be taken by the Free State soldiers, the men inside were instructed by phone to destroy the building and retreat to the Glentworth Hotel, but they were captured by Free State soldiers advancing through the sewers under the streets before they could manage to do this. Brennan's troops had now secured a key position, a major foothold from which they could drive the IRA from the docks.

Despite the Free State army's success here, IRA volunteers in William Street continued to fight, launching a sniping attack on the Free State army headquarters in William Street police barracks and wounding two Free State officers as they entered the building. The republicans also had some success in inflicting casualties on Free State units in Cannock's tower, Quin's of Thomas Street and Henry Street.

At 8.10 p.m. on Friday, the Free State army attacked the Castle barracks with armoured cars, but withdrew after ten minutes when machine-gun fire proved useless against the great stone walls of the ancient stone fortress. The attack was probably launched with a view to keeping up morale on the Free State side, while trying to mount the pressure on the Castle's defenders, rather than with any serious hope of victory. A similarly fruitless attack occurred two hours later, when the Free State army attacked Ryan's corner of Roches Street with two armoured cars in an attempt to gain back the territory that the IRA had won from them the day before. The machine-gun fire of the armoured cars blew in the steel shutters the IRA had erected on the windows for protection. The republicans inside retreated into the shop next door, but returned to Ryan's corner without casualties when the Free State armoured cars withdrew to their barracks.

At this point the mayor of Limerick, disturbed by the extent and intensity of the fighting, issued a proclamation calling on civilians to evacuate Carey's Road, Edward Street, Wolfe Tone Street and the area surrounding the New barracks.

Outside the city the IRA had blown up bridges north of Ennis in an attempt to disrupt troop transports bringing reinforcements to the Free State forces in Limerick. All trains from Ennis were stopped and the roads had been blocked, but this failed to stop the Free State advance.

SATURDAY 15 JULY

In Clare the IRA took advantage of the absence of Michael Brennan's Free State troops by launching attacks against Free State positions. On 15 July two Free State officers, Captain Lynch and Lieutenant Roche, travelling to a conference by car, were sniped at by IRA volunteers. The bullets shattered the car's windscreen and one even struck the steering wheel, but both men escaped unharmed. The same day the IRA launched an offensive against Free State-held barracks and positions in towns and villages through the West and Mid Clare Brigade areas. The republicans had already destroyed bridges at Droicheadnagower and Claureen, and were preparing to detonate a mine under Latoon bridge on the main Ennis–Limerick road, when they were surprised by a company of Free State soldiers and had to withdraw, leaving the bridge intact. When darkness fell the IRA began attacks on Free State barracks in the west of the county. They succeeded in capturing the towns of Kilrush and Kilkee, but not without losses. During the attack on Kilrush, IRA volunteer Patrick O'Dea was shot dead. Two days later, on 17 July, IRA volunteer Seán O'Halloran was killed in action fighting against Free State troops at Bunahow between Gort and Ennis.

To effectively hold the territory they had taken, the IRA needed to keep Clare isolated from Free State forces in Limerick, Dublin and the midlands. Thus, the republicans began tearing up tracks and removing wooden sleepers on railway lines throughout Clare and soon no trains were travelling to or from Ennis on either the West Clare or Great Southern Railways.

In Limerick city, the Free State army felt confident enough on the morning of 15 July to launch an attack on the two IRA-held barracks on the north-western side of the city, the Castle and Strand barracks. Their confidence arose from the fact that the SS *Arovina* had by now reached Limerick with reinforcements, equipment and supplies for the troops under Brennan's command.

Connie McNamara, commander of the Strand barracks, had been in involved in IRA attacks on several RIC police barracks during the War of Independence, including John's Street, Murroe and Kilmallock barracks in Limerick, and Rearcross barracks in Tipperary. He now hoped to use his experience of the assault and defence of smaller police barracks to defend the much larger Strand barracks from attack by the Free State soldiers. In preparation for a siege he had stockpiled food, cigarettes and ammunition to supply the sixty-five men under his command. The IRA had also established a Red Cross field hospital beside the barracks.

On the evening of 15 July, the Free State army launched simultaneous attacks on the Castle and Strand barracks attacking the IRA in both buildings with armoured cars, grenades, machine-guns and mortar fire. At Strand barracks, the Free State armoured cars raked the front of the building with machine-gun fire and mortar crews rained a bombardment on the republicans inside as a distraction, while a mine-laying party led by Captain Hessian advanced. Hessian was a native of Galway and a former member of the Connacht Rangers in the British army. At one point the soldiers under Hessian's command had advanced so close to the Strand barracks that they almost managed to place a mine against its rear wall. However, the IRA garrison inside concentrated heavy fire on this party and the Free State soldiers were driven back before they could place or detonate the mine. The republicans across the river in the Castle barracks were also successful in repulsing the Free State attacks. The Free State troops were eventually forced to withdraw and plan some other course of action to capture the barracks.

The attempt to lay a mine at the rear of the Strand barracks was an imitation of an IRA tactic used in the War of Independence to attack RIC barracks. The idea was that if the defenders of a barracks came under rifle and machine-gun fire, they would be kept busy at the barracks' windows fighting off their attackers. Then, when the mine detonated, blowing a breach in the building's defences, a storming party kept in readiness could rush through the gap and fight their way into the building and capture it. However, Connie McNamara's experience in the War of Independence meant that he was familiar with this tactic and was able to successfully deploy the men under his command to force back the Free State storming party and the group who were advancing with the mine. By the close of the day, the attacks on the Strand and Castle barracks had failed.

SUNDAY 16 JULY

At 5.30 a.m. the following morning the Free State army launched another attack on the Strand barracks, this time hoping that their early morning assault would enable them to take McNamara's men inside by surprise. Under cover of rifle and machine-gun fire from the courthouse, custom house, Cruise's Hotel and St Mary's tower on the opposite side of the Shannon, two Free State armoured cars and an armour-plated Lancia lorry managed to smash through the republican defences and dash along Strand Road to the front of the barracks. The two armoured cars kept pouring barrages of machine-gun fire into the front of the barracks from the centre of the road in an effort to provide cover for the soldiers in the lorry, who began throwing buckets of petrol and paraffin against the wooden barracks' gate and at the windows. At the same time another group of soldiers began an attack on the rear of the barracks using grenades. They had some success and at one point the attackers managed to fight their way into a house adjoining the barracks. The Free State soldiers at the barracks' gate managed to ignite the petrol and set part of the front of the barracks on fire, but they were soon driven back by the IRA volunteers inside using Thompson and Vickers machine-guns. Finally, after a bitterly contested battle lasting half an hour, the republicans managed to drive off the attack, and the Free State army, realising that their second effort was doomed to failure, withdrew their vehicles from Strand Road and their soldiers from the rear of the barracks.

In the city centre the IRA sent their improvised armoured car, 'The Hooded Terror', from the New barracks to attack Free State positions in William Street. The vehicle moved slowly through the town down Catherine Street and made it as far as the junction of Thomas Street without encountering any resistance – it is likely that any Free State soldiers who saw it presumed the armoured car was one of their own vehicles. 'The Hooded Terror' was forced to halt by a barricade thrown across Thomas Street. At this point any possible confusion about the ownership of the vehicle in the minds of the watching Free State soldiers was immediately dispelled, when the IRA volunteers inside opened fire on the soldiers stationed at Patrick O'Halloran's drapery shop on William Street. The vehicle's Hotchkiss machine-gun sent twenty round bursts of tracer bullets from its barrel crashing into the shop front, wounding two of the Free State soldiers inside and setting the stock stored there on fire.

The firefight continued until the IRA volunteer manning the Hotchkiss gun ran out of ammunition and the armoured car turned slowly in the street, still under fire, and made its way back towards the New barracks. Within a few minutes of the car's departure, the Free State troops came out from behind their cover and managed to extinguish the fire, with the help of a party of their comrades who had rushed to the scene from William Street police barracks.

Later that evening Michael Brennan ordered an attack on the IRA volunteers who had taken over O'Mara's Bacon Factory. Brennan's men managed to inflict some casualties on the republicans there, but like all other attacks launched that day, they were driven back by their opponents without gaining any territory. Sniping was intense along the docks, and on Roches Street, William Street, Catherine Street, O'Connell Street and Henry Street.

In the midst of all this fighting, the city's bread delivery vans managed to make short delivery runs to some of the poorer quarters of the city:

> In the midst of the hottest fire, food distribution went on undisturbed from day to day. Bread van and milk car drivers took their lives in their hands as they passed along, and their quiet heroism saved many a family from actual want.[64]

> The plight of the inhabitants is becoming desperate. All who could get away have already done so. Many people have not seen members of their families for several days, and the greatest anxiety prevails as a consequence.[65]

MONDAY 17 JULY

Unimpressed with the failure to dislodge the IRA from Limerick, O'Duffy left Dublin with reinforcements and arrived in Limerick on Monday 17 July to take command of Free State army operations in Limerick himself. O'Duffy and his troops travelled across the midlands. A force of about forty IRA volunteers were occupying a handful of houses on either side of the bridge spanning the Shannon between Ballina and Killaloe. They were routed by Free State troops from Nenagh and O'Briens Bridge shortly before O'Duffy's main force reached the town, and he established his headquarters at the Lakeside Hotel in Killaloe on the banks of the Shannon just sixteen miles up the river from Limerick city.

By now John Pinkman and the other members of Tom Flood's Free State column were nearing the city for what they hoped would be the final push needed to run the republicans out of Limerick:

> Early the next morning we boarded the lorries again and set out for Ballina and then on to Killaloe where we were to stay that night. The main road was frequently blocked by trees cut down by the Irregulars, and we often had to stop in order to clear a path for the vehicles in the convoy. In some places the road was so heavily blocked that we were forced to detour through the side roads. Even these were sometimes impassable, and rather than allow ourselves to be delayed until all the trees were cleared, we had no choice but to get out of the lorries and leg it.
>
> Occasionally a shot was fired at us from across the fields and then one or two of us would chase off in the direction from which the shot came. One of our lads, a Tipperary fellow who joined us at Nenagh as a sort of guide, could run like a hare, and the moment he heard a shot he'd leap out over the hedge and tear off after the padjoe.[66] He was just an ordinary country lad, but

that Tipperary fellow, whose name I believe was Coppinger, had lots of real courage and I was glad when I heard several months later that he had been promoted to the rank of lieutenant. The Irregulars, however, weren't a serious problem except for the occasional sniper; whenever they saw us coming they fled into the countryside without attempting to shoot it out. Judging from the report of their rifles, most of the snipers were armed with Mausers which had a distinctive 'snap' when fired.

It was a beautiful morning as we marched into Killaloe on the road along the banks of the River Shannon. The sun shone across the waters and over the loveliest of green hills and meadows. For a while I didn't think the scene could be made more perfect: and then I heard the church bells ringing for morning mass. When the other lads saw how entranced I was with this peaceful scene of lovely Irish countryside, some of them teased me about it. But I didn't care, for I felt I was the High King of Ireland.

Shortly after arriving in Killaloe we were assigned to various billets in the town and I was one of a party sent to a big house that resembled a small private hotel. In the afternoon I took the opportunity of visiting the famous waterfalls because I wasn't sure of how long we'd remain in Killaloe. After tea that evening I went in search of a fellow named White who'd been a great friend of mine in Dartmoor prison. I hadn't seen him since the time of his release until the night we pulled into Nenagh when I spotted him climbing out of a Tender full of troops. We were delighted to see each other again, but our reunion was short-lived because our two groups were separated for the night. We had just enough time to vow that when we got to Killaloe we'd get together again and have a night on the town.

I roamed around the town checking the various billets in hope of finding White, but without success. Then I met one of my own crowd who'd been assigned to do guard duty that night, but who begged me to stand in for him. He was a Dubliner and said he had a brother, or cousin, living in Killaloe whom he hadn't seen in years and might not see again for a long time. I felt sorry for him and knew he'd do the same for me if I were in his situation, so I agreed. Anyway it was too late for me to continue looking for White, although there was a possibility that I might meet him if he came through the street while I was on sentry duty.

I finished a two-hour spell of guard duty at midnight, but White never turned up and I turned in when my relief took over. It seemed as if I'd just got nicely settled down for forty winks when the sound of a shot rang out in the night. The entire picket turned out to investigate, and we soon learned that the sentry had fired at someone creeping along in the dark street. After a quick search we came across a figure huddled up on the ground close to the walls of an old house. When we turned him over to take a good look at him, we saw he'd been shot through the head. It was White. O Jesus! My heart nearly broke when I saw the poor fellow lying there dead. Everyone felt terrible about it especially when they learned he'd been with me in Dartmoor.

In the morning I got the full story of the tragedy. When we failed to find each other the previous evening, White had gone off in search of a friend of his in Killaloe and the two of them got drunk on poitín. Returning late at night full of drink, White was shot as he was trying to find his billet by the sentry who mistook him for an infiltrator. Of course nobody blamed the sentry, any of us would have done the same thing. Our officers had warned us that we were in Irregular territory and the picket had been instructed to take no chances. The sentry couldn't have seen that White was in fact one of our own soldiers, because it was a very dark night and in those days none of the Irish country towns had street lighting.

From that day until this – although God knows I've had a thousand opportunities to do so – I have never touched a drop of poitín.[67]

TUESDAY 18 JULY

Upon receiving news of the imminent arrival of O'Duffy's forces, the IRA in Limerick launched an offensive on Michael Brennan's Free State troops in the William Street area of the city centre, hoping this time to drive them from the city centre before O'Duffy's column could reinforce them.

The republicans' main attack on Tuesday 18 July was spearheaded by fifty IRA volunteers who made their way towards William Street on foot. As both sides suffered from a shortage of uniforms, this IRA unit wore red armbands on their sleeves in an attempt to distinguish friend from foe in the fighting. They moved forward crouching low in small groups, ten feet apart, on both sides of the street and managed to make their way unchallenged along Edward Street, Parnell Street and downhill to Roches Street and Thomas Street. Their hobnailed boots were often fouled as they manoeuvred through the sewage from the townspeople's chamber pots which they had emptied into the street from their windows rather than risk venturing outside and being caught in the crossfire. From Thomas Street they attempted to fight their way down the narrow laneway at Fox's Bow, but were driven back by machine-gun and rifle fire from two sides as the Free State troops at William Street and in the Strand Cottage on the northern bank of the Shannon, 300 yards away, who had a clear line of fire straight up Shannon Street and Roches Street, opened fire. As they attempted to take cover and mount another attack, a party of Free State soldiers rushed from William Street through Fox's Bow and forced them to retreat. As the IRA volunteers fell back down Roches Street their comrades could not open fire on the advancing Free State troops as the two groups were now so close together they risked killing and wounding their own men in the process. Because of this the Free State soldiers managed to gain a foothold in Roches Street and, after summoning reinforcements from William Street, gained control of it after a short battle.

WEDNESDAY 19 JULY

By Wednesday the main section of Eoin O'Duffy's forces, concentrated to the north of Limerick city in Nenagh, County Tipperary, and Killaloe in east Clare, were ready to break through the remaining IRA units scattered between them and the city, and force their way into Limerick city.

On O'Connell Street the IRA occupied Kidd's Café. The Free State soldiers could now only cross the street in relative safety from Cruise's Hotel to their post on the opposite side of the street by using a trench they had cut across the street with a barricade erected beside it facing Arthur's Quay. From Kidd's Café the IRA sniped O'Connell Street with Mauser rifles unhindered, as Free State armoured cars were unable to break through republican barricades to mount an attack. Starting in the basement of a building on the William Street–O'Connell Street corner, the Free State troops began tunnelling towards Kidd's Café to deal with this problem. They broke a passage through each building using picks, sledgehammers and crowbars, usually using fireplaces as weak points of entry. Eventually they managed to tunnel right into the basement of Kidd's Café. The IRA men inside were taken by surprise and after a brief firefight were forced to retreat to the Glentworth Hotel. The Free State forces now had full control of O'Connell Street from the Town Hall to the O'Connell monument, a distance of 400 yards.

In the battle for control of this area, IRA volunteer Paddy Naughton was mortally wounded by a Free State sniper. He died in the arms of his comrade Connie Neenan:

> We lost a couple of great lads there. One fellow that I recall now, Paddy Naughton, he was very good in the Tan War. We were crossing O'Connell Street separately when he was hit. He fell. I helped him up and pushed him through a door. Paddy, I said, you are all right, we will take care of you. But he turned his eyes up to me, Connie will you look after my rifle? Nonsense, Paddy, I replied, that's a superficial wound. But I saw then that his consciousness was going from him. Dear Christ, but he was a terrific man at a time when we needed men.[68]

With the failure of the IRA's offensive, Mayor Stephen O'Mara issued a second notice calling on civilians living near the city's barracks to evacuate their homes because of the danger of artillery bombardment. In response, thousands of refugees left the city seeking shelter in Clarina and Adare. Some of the people of Limerick even fled as far away as Nenagh in County Tipperary in search of safety. With the imminent arrival of Free State artillery, Connie McNamara knew that his command in the Strand barracks would be one of the first buildings to be targeted. With a huge burden of responsibility on his shoulders for the defence of the barracks and the lives of the sixty-five men under his command, he ordered his younger brother Thomas to leave the barracks. Perhaps the realisation that he and other members of the garrison could be dead within a few days if not hours, the possibility that his parents would have to mourn the loss of both sons was too much to contemplate, so he transferred Thomas to a safer post.

On King's Island the Free State soldiers held the courthouse, St Mary's cathedral, a pub on the corner of Nicholas Street–Athlunkard Street, Mary Street police barracks and Healy's house at Park bridge. They also controlled three of the four bridges connecting the island with the rest of the city; the fourth – Thomond bridge – was controlled from the Castle barracks and IRA positions on the northern bank of the Shannon. Although the forces of the two armies were almost evenly matched in this area, with about 100 troops on each side, by operating a Lewis machine-gun from the bell tower of St Mary's and by occasional sniper attacks, the Free State troops were able to advance slowly and steadily towards the Castle barracks. However, without reinforcements they could not hope to capture it and had to settle for harassing and pinning down the IRA garrison inside.

Realising that, with the arrival of O'Duffy's troops in the vicinity, their forces were being surrounded and that the Strand barracks was their key position, the IRA leaders at the Castle barracks issued orders to move as many men as possible to the Strand barracks to reinforce the garrison there. Men were smuggled out of the Castle using a Red Cross ambulance to carry them the short journey to the Red Cross field hospital beside the Strand barracks. Having watched the ambulance make several such journeys, the Free State soldiers stationed in the tower of St Mary's cathedral became suspicious. When the ambulance stalled, and two men got out to push it, the Free State soldiers opened fire on the ambulance with their Lewis gun, much to the horror of the civilians watching from the windows of their houses overlooking the drama.

Sniping attacks and occasional charges by Free State armoured cars, their machine-guns sending hails of bullets towards the IRA garrison inside, came every few hours, depriving the Strand barracks defenders of sleep and rest. However, during a lull in the fighting, the IRA volunteers under McNamara's command managed to rebuild the barricades surrounding their position and at the barracks' gates. With raw and bloodied hands they scraped through the rubble, dust and splintered wood for material to reinforce their defences. They also managed to tunnel into the neighbouring houses to set up new defences, the weary bloodshot workers stumbling over each other under the weight of bricks and stones, before making their way back to the sandbagged windows to take up their rifles and await the next attack.

Desperately in need of some tactical advantage that would turn the tide in the battle for Limerick city before

O'Duffy's reinforcements arrived, the IRA came up with a plan to use a fire engine to spray petrol or paraffin on William Street police barracks and destroy the building by fire, forcing the Free State army headquarters in the city to surrender. However, the only fire engine that was suitable for the operation had been moved from Limerick to County Cork some weeks earlier. The IRA wrote to Lynch outlining their plans and pleading that it should be brought back to Limerick for the proposed attack immediately.

To C/S, F.GHQ Fermoy.

1. The Leyland Motor Fire Engine, was exhibited in Limerick about six weeks ago. It works directly from a hydrant, therefore would work from a barrel, and throws water 900ft and 300ft high. It can travel at a speed of from 50 to 60 miles per hour. It could be protected, and worked from the position now held by our men in Limerick, and might be employed in burning out Wm St Barracks.
2. This engine is believed to be somewhere in Cork at present.
3. Will you please try to have it located.[69]

On the same day the republicans issued a new propaganda news sheet, which included an appeal to the Irish people to join them in resisting the Free State army and rejecting the Treaty:

You are told that the Free Staters want one country – one government. Yet they, by the acceptance of this so-called Treaty, sanction the cutting up of our country by the Welsh Wizard [British Prime Minister Lloyd George], and the setting up of a bigoted Orange government in the Six Counties whose sole object is the clearing out of the Catholic minority, and making Belfast and the rest of the Six Counties safe for English democracy.

There must be no misunderstanding as to our present stand, and the public must realise that the conflict that has been forced upon us at England's bidding is going to be of long duration before they see the destruction of the republic which Tone, Emmet, Pearse and the other Irish martyrs set out to establish.[70]

That night O'Duffy's Free State troops began pouring into the city from Killaloe. The main body, led by Commandant Dennis Galvin, reached Limerick city at 10 p.m. on Wednesday 19 July. Galvin's column included four truck-loads of soldiers, a Whippet armoured car, two Lancia armoured vehicles, 400 rifles, ten Lewis machine-guns, 400 grenades and 50,000 rounds of ammunition. In addition to this the convoy included an 18-pounder artillery field gun nicknamed 'Seán MacEoin's 18-pounder'. More than any other weaponry or supplies that O'Duffy brought, this field gun would decide the outcome of the battle in Limerick city. Towed behind a lorry at a slow but steady speed of about nine miles per hour, it crossed the Shannon at Corbally bridge and came over the Abbey bridge into the city centre where it was set up at Arthur's Quay, directly across the river from the Strand barracks.

THURSDAY 20 JULY

The Free State army launched another direct attack on the rear of the Strand barracks. Not only did the IRA men inside manage to resist this attack, but they also managed to damage and immobilise one of the Free State's armoured cars. Surprised at the dogged resistance from the republican defenders of the Strand barracks, O'Duffy's newly arrived troops took charge of the operation and decided to use their 18-pounder field gun to shell the building, reduce it to rubble and collapse not only the barracks' 4-foot thick stone walls, but also the spirit of the garrison inside.

The gun was set up alongside the mills on Custom House Quay, 40 feet behind the quay wall, its barrel aimed at the Strand barracks just 200 yards away. Amongst its crew were four Limerick men: Colonel Fraher, Jim Leddin and brothers John and Michael McNamara, who had all served in the Royal Artillery in the British army during the First World War. By now news of the gun's arrival had spread far and wide through the city and large crowds of civilians gathered to see it wreak its destruction.

At 10 a.m. a republican prisoner advanced from the Free

State positions holding aloft a white flag and proceeded to the barracks with a message from Michael Brennan. The message gave McNamara and his men five minutes to surrender before the building would be shelled. As the prisoner delivered the message and was conferring with McNamara, he was shot and badly wounded by a sniper. McNamara refused to surrender and sent two nurses from the Red Cross field hospital across Sarsfield bridge to Cruise's Hotel with the reply that he 'would not surrender while he still had ammunition or cover'.

Shortly before 10.30 a.m. the gun was prepared for use. A few minutes later the first shot was fired at the barracks from 'Seán MacEoin's 18-pounder'. The first shell sailed through the air and struck a telegraph pole 30 feet to the left of the barracks. It cut the pole in half and ricocheted to the right, crashing into the second window to the right of the gate at the front of the barracks, and skidding and skipping along Strand Road before finally coming to a halt at the foot of the Treaty Stone. The roar of the explosion and the force of the recoil caused the gun to leap a foot and a half into the air before skidding back over the cobblestones scattering the gun crew. The British army had faced the same problems when they first used mounted artillery pieces, designed for the mud of disputed countryside rather than city streets, to shell the GPO in 1916.

Recovering from their shock the gun crew repositioned the gun, hastily digging a shallow hole for the foot plate of the gun through the cobbled road surface to prevent it moving again and fired a second shot. This time the shell scored a direct hit on the front of the barracks, blowing the barracks' gates from their hinges. But again the gun came loose from the recoil and was thrown so far back that it swung sideways and one of its wheels became stuck in the hole dug for the foot plate. Once more the gun was dragged forward and manhandled into position.

The bombardment continued for over an hour and in total nineteen shells were fired, battering a huge hole in the front wall of the barracks. 'The front gate was blown away with a shell and two large holes forged in the masonry work, one of which was sufficient to admit a horse and cart to pass through.'[71] However, the IRA volunteers defending the barracks remained defiant and the Free State soldiers now had the laborious task, whilst under fire, of moving the field gun across the Shannon and repositioning it behind the barracks where the shelling recommenced. In response to the bombardment the IRA garrison withdrew further into the building, sniping through the dust and sunlight billowing around the breaches in the front of the barracks at the Free State positions on the other bank of the Shannon. They still refused to surrender and continually repaired their barricades and erected new defences in expectation of a direct assault.

Meanwhile the IRA units in other parts of the city, upon hearing the shelling, realised what was happening and attempted to break through the Free State lines to come to the aid of McNamara and his men. They advanced steadily up O'Connell Street before being driven back by machine-gun fire from the troops at the northern ends of both Thomas Street and William Street. The *Irish Times* correspondent in the city described the fighting as: 'A furious duel … where outposts faced each other in opposite houses. In some lanes where windows were not five yards apart, grenades were frequently thrown.'[72]

Having withstood a second barrage from the rear of the building, time was now running out for the beleaguered republicans in the Strand barracks. At around 7 p.m., after shells from 'Sean MacEoin's 18-pounder' tore a gaping hole in the rear wall of the barracks, Free State soldiers led by Colonel David Reynolds and armed with a large supply of grenades, attempted to storm the breach in the north-eastern corner of the barracks. On entering the breach they met a wall of intense gunfire from the IRA men inside. Colonel Reynolds was badly wounded and Captain Con O'Halloran from Ennis was hit in the chest by a burst of fire from a Thompson machine-gun, one of the bullets piercing his right lung, before the storming party was driven back. However, most of the remaining IRA men inside realised that it was only a matter of time before the Free State army captured the barracks. Many quickly made their way to the Red Cross field hospital next door and from there escaped down back lanes and across the fields towards the Clare hills. A fire had broken out in the barracks and the remaining defenders were pinned down by heavy machine-gun fire. McNamara realised that he could not realistically hold out for much longer. To preserve the lives of the last twenty-two men under his command, he decided to surrender.

During the attack, the Free State troops had failed to cut the telephone wires to the barracks, which allowed McNamara to negotiate his surrender by phone. While he was speaking on the phone agreeing to terms, a bullet from a Free State sniper blew the receiver out of his hand, missing his head by inches. With the surrender agreed the remaining IRA men received the final order from McNamara to destroy their weapons rather than let them fall into the hands of the enemy, and they set to work smashing them against walls and flinging their remaining ammunition into the Shannon, while awaiting the arrival of the Free State troops. The IRA volunteers in the barracks flew a white flour bag mounted on a broom handle from the top right-hand window of the building as a makeshift flag of surrender. At 8 p.m. McNamara and his men formally surrendered when Lieutenant Barry led a Free State force into the barracks. Brennan complimented them on their defence and offered McNamara a commission as an officer in the Free State army, serving on Brennan's personal staff, if he would change his allegiance. As could be expected from a man who had fought such a dogged resistance for his principles, McNamara refused and instead marched off across Sarsfield bridge to imprisonment in William Street police barracks with his men.

The flour bag remained flying from the Strand barracks which *The Irish Times* would describe on Sunday 23 July as: 'a palsied pile, a grim tribute to the accuracy of the national artillery'. That night the flour bag was taken down by Captain Hessian, the officer who had led the party attempting to mine the back of the barracks a few days earlier. Upon taking it down he used a piece of charcoal to write 'Strand Barrack. Thursday 20 July' on his treasured souvenir. Now the Free State had undisputed control of the north bank of the Shannon and both Thomond and Sarsfield bridges.

With the surrender of Connie McNamara's men in the Strand barracks, the Free State army immediately switched their attention towards the Castle barracks. They moved the 18-pounder field artillery gun into a new position and began shelling the building. During the shelling some of the barracks buildings inside the Castle courtyard caught fire. Whether this was a result of the shelling, or whether the fire was started deliberately by the IRA garrison stationed there is not certain. IRA commandant, Stephen Kennedy, who was in charge of the Castle barracks garrison, ordered the remaining IRA volunteers inside to retreat. However, as they attempted to withdraw from the Castle, they found themselves almost completely surrounded and had to be rescued by a group of local fishermen who rowed across the Shannon to the Castle walls, unnoticed by Free State soldiers on the opposite bank. Kennedy then led his men out of the city. Later that evening they were able to link up with a larger force of the IRA's Mid Limerick Brigade in Tipperary.

That evening Liam Lynch ordered the IRA to evacuate the barracks they still held and to retreat southwards, after burning the buildings to prevent the Free State army occupying them. According to Liam Deasy: 'He must have realised the futility of opposing artillery in street fighting and he ordered a general withdrawal.'[73]

Shortly after midnight the IRA garrison at the New barracks evacuated in a convoy of cars along the Ballinacurra road. As they left the barracks the few remaining IRA volunteers covered their retreat with machine-gun fire, keeping the advancing Free State soldiers who were attempting to encircle the barracks and trap the republicans inside. The main group headed south towards Kilmallock and Bruree, only stopping briefly every few miles to fell trees across the roads, plant landmines and demolish bridges with explosives to slow any Free State troops advancing behind them.

The remaining IRA fighters used passages they had broken from house to house to retreat unseen through the houses in the city centre, still firing an occasional shot at the Free State positions and occasionally stopping now and then to mount a fresh sniping attack. Shortly before midnight there was a noticeable lull in the fighting and a large convoy of motor vehicles commandeered by the IRA left the city by the only available escape route, the Ballinacurra road. As a covering action for this retreat, intense rifle and machine-gun fire was directed against Free State positions around Military Road.

The IRA volunteers in the New barracks immediately began dousing the inside of each barrack building with petrol and paraffin, and setting them on fire to deny their Free State enemies the use of a strategic building from which they could control the city. At 12.30 p.m. three huge mine explosions rocked the Military Road entrance of the New barracks, partially demolishing the gateway and blocking it with rubble. The explosions were so powerful that they sent stones, brick and other debris crashing through the roofs of houses on Wolfe Tone Street and the surrounding area. Connie Neenan remembered:

> We were in a tight situation and in the end we had no chance against them. Retreat became inevitable. My strongest complaint is that we were ordered out at an early hour of the evening while it was still daylight. That made it all the harder. The retreat when it came resembled a stampede. We were the last to leave the New barracks; it was a scene of chaos, everyone was gone. We were so hungry I went out and stole a loaf of bread.[74]

The very last group to leave the New barracks with Liam Deasy, as the fire took hold and every building became a blazing inferno, were the women of Cumann na mBan led by Madge Daly:

The republican forces in the New barracks were joined by Cumann na mBan who helped them in many ways. The hospital was in the charge of Nurse Laffan and Nurse Connerty, a Limerick girl home from New York on holiday. These nurses, with the nursing section of Cumann na mBan, attended to the sick and wounded, whilst other girls helped with the cooking of meals and maintenance. When the republicans evacuated the city, the girls remained in the barracks until the men had got clear, and then returned to their homes, still ready to undertake any duty required of them.[75]

Connie Neenan recorded:

And so we fell back through Patrickswell, Adare, finally ending up in Buttevant about four o'clock in the morning. We felt hopelessly disillusioned and disheartened. The whole flaming struggle seemed to be leading nowhere. They captured our men, held them and later shot some of them. We captured their men, sometimes twice over, and had to let them go. We had nowhere to put them, no arrangements. No one had the heart to fight.[76]

The retreating republicans fought a well-conducted rearguard action, making good use of covering machine-gun fire. They withdrew as far as the Kilmallock–Bruree area in County Limerick, where they began setting up a defensive position, expecting an advance and attack by the Free State army as soon as they had consolidated their hold on Limerick city and re-organised their forces. The republicans were unchallenged by the few Free State troops in their path as they retreated through the countryside, except at Crossagalla, where an IRA volunteer called Slattery was killed.

CHAPTER 6

THE END OF THE CONFLICT IN LIMERICK CITY

The first indication to the city's inhabitants and the Free State soldiers that the republicans had retreated was the brilliant illumination of the night's sky directly over the New and Ordnance barracks. The alarm was raised for the fire brigade and people in nearby houses crowded into the streets, oblivious to any remaining danger, to watch the buildings being consumed by fire. It was a fine night with a gentle summer's breeze and any immediate fears that the fires would spread and engulf the citizen's homes were soon allayed.

The fires blazed fiercest in the New barracks and were watched by a large crowd outside the main barracks' gate and by a few more adventurous onlookers who were brave or foolish enough to venture inside the complex and watch the destruction from the sprawling barrack square. By two o'clock on the morning of Friday 21 July, almost the entire complex was engulfed in the blaze. The commanding officers' quarters, the western block of soldiers' accommodation, the gym, the officers' mess, the hospital and the recreation block were completely destroyed. Only a portion of the soldiers' quarters on the eastern side of the barracks, the married soldiers' quarters and the detention barracks escaped the flames. The clock overlooking the barracks square stopped at 2.30 a.m., a silent witness looming over the destruction below.

Soon the silent crowds of civilians who had stood by, passively watching the building being engulfed by the flames, were spurred to action by a compulsion to profit from the destruction of the barracks. Their main interest was in stores of food, but everything which could be removed – fire grates, stoves, corrugated iron torn from sheds and also large quantities of furniture – was taken away before sunrise. According to Tony McMahon, who was a young boy at the time:

> Throughout the night, heavily laden men and women streamed from the gates with furniture, army blankets, bedding provisions and food stuffs. Groups came down Barrack Hill staggering under heavy bags and awkward pieces of equipment and

furniture. One man had a sack of flour on his back that weighed very heavily on him as he tottered out the gate. On the hill he remarked that he was getting used to the load and the incline down helped a lot. He planned to go up later for another bag. As he reached the level ground he began to wonder about how light the bag weight had become and looking back up the hill he saw a white trail of flour and then looked at the slack bag on his back. Some 'friend' had ripped a hole in the bag with a knife. The language of the disappointed man was unprintable, but not inaudible. In the barrack square there were motor vans and trucks. On one van was the name of the firm J&G Boyd Ltd. New motor cycles were still in their brown wrapping covers. A dreaded Crossley Tender, still with the wire netting 'cage' stood abandoned. Many an adult viewed and inspected it at close range for the first time – a year earlier when it careered through the city streets carrying its heavily armed Auxiliaries and Tans, people cleared for safety out of its way.[77]

The Ordnance barracks was completely destroyed and the garrison retreated from the city. The Frederick Street barracks, which had also been held by the IRA, was set on fire by members of Na Fianna Éireann, but before the fires could take hold they were put out by people from the surrounding houses who were afraid that the blaze would ignite the nearby Gas Works and the Electric Lighting Power House. When they spotted the first flames licking the brickwork from the upper windows of the barracks, the street's residents managed to find two fire hoses and half a dozen men from the locality forced the barracks door open and rushed inside to douse the flames. The rest of the residents formed an amateur fire brigade using not just buckets but chamber pots, saucepans and every available vessel to bring water to the scene. The fire was put out before any major damage was done.

The outbreak of the simultaneous fires across the city's barracks was the signal to the Free State army that their enemy had fled and that, for the meantime, the fighting was over. The sounds of battle were replaced with the peal of church bells on King's Island when the Free State soldiers stationed on the roof and bell tower of St Mary's cathedral realised what was happening. 'The bells of St Mary's Protestant church rang out on Friday night while the fires raged in the four fortresses which had been occupied by the Irregulars. The national troops rang a peal to announce to the citizens that the Irregulars [IRA] had left the city.'[78] The Free State soldiers moved cautiously from their posts, advancing slowly towards the barracks set ablaze by the republicans to inspect the damage. They travelled at a slow pace in small groups, crunching the shattered window glass that lay on the streets as they ventured through the dark with their rifles at the ready. If the republicans had really evacuated the whole city then the men of the Free State army were in no rush to pursue them. After ten days of heavy fighting they would now be glad of a rest and to be allowed to savour the taste of victory, before engaging in battle again. They were also wary of possible attacks from republican snipers who might still be in position, watching them from the rooftops, or stragglers from the republican evacuation who were lagging behind in the hope of firing a few parting shots at their enemy.

Private John Pinkman and the other Free State soldiers in Tom Flood's column were advancing on the city at daybreak when news reached them of the republican retreat:

Our departure from Killaloe was delayed for a couple of days until reinforcements of additional troops and lorries joined us for the move to Limerick. When we were within two or three miles of the city, Captain Tom Flood, the O/C of our flying column, called a halt to tell us that the Irregulars had been driven out of Limerick, but that they might be waiting to ambush us as we advanced along the road. We then spread out across neighbouring fields and, keeping a safe watch for signs of ambush, we cleared the way for the main convoy driving slowly down the road behind us. As we reached the outskirts of Limerick, Tom Flood called us all together and we marched through the city in regular company formation.

Although Limerick had been cleared of the Irregulars, there was considerable evidence of the fierce ten day fight that had taken place before our arrival; some of the barricades were still on the streets, and when we went to Cruise's Hotel, our intended headquarters, we found it a shambles. Some women volunteers made tea and sandwiches for us in the hotel's kitchen before we were split up and sent off to various billets. I found myself in a party billeted at the commercial hotel.[79]

Pinkman and his comrades weren't the only ones in the city to find new lodgings. Tony McMahon, who had witnessed some of the worst fighting in the Military Road area, remembered that as soon as the fighting had ended, families from the city's slums began squatting in the former accommodation of the British army officers who had left the city months before, now that they were certain no military force would evict them at a moment's notice to set up an outpost or a sniping position:

When the British army left Limerick for the last time the residential quarters of the officers in Clare Street and the Crescent were vacated, but only for a very short time. Families from dangerous and condemned houses from the slums moved in with their battered furniture, old bedding and a few personal belongings, but with swarms of children of all ages. The exclusive residential Crescent had been transformed overnight – the quality of life radically changed. Palliasses, blankets, sheets and washing hung airing and drying in the morning air from the front windows of the converted flats on every storey of the Georgian houses. Children played on the steps and swung from the bars; women loudly greeted neighbours from window to window and engaged in long chats.[80]

The total cost of destruction during the ten days of fighting in Limerick city was estimated at £250,000. The Office of Public Works estimated the cost of repairing the damage caused by shelling of the Strand barracks at £1,400 and the burning of the New barracks by the IRA at £10,000. However, the worst of the destruction had been confined to the city's police and military barracks, and the *Irish Times* correspondent in the city reported that most of the city centre was relatively unscathed by the fighting:

> In view of the length and intensity of the hostilities, the wonder is that so little damage was done. Apart from wholesale looting, most of the commercial concerns have come through the ordeal almost unscathed. Ranges of the plate glass frontages in the centre of the firing zone remain intact. But corner premises in commanding positions are badly chipped by gunfire.[81]

O'Duffy described the battle for Limerick as 'the finest operation in the present war' in a letter to Michael Collins.[82] However, in a report to Richard Mulcahy he described the Free State troops who had been under his command in Limerick in less glorious terms:

> We had to get work out of a disorganised, indisciplined and cowardly crowd. Arms were handed over wholesale to the enemy, sentries were drunk at their posts and when a whole garrison was put in the clink owing to insubordination, etc.

> the garrison sent to replace them often turned out to be worse
> ... 300 'duds' were sent here from the Curragh, who had never
> handled a rifle until they came here. Half of those are now in
> [the] clink, or have deserted altogether.[83]

The damage in terms of loss of life in Limerick far outweighed any monetary cost. At least five republicans, six Free State soldiers and eleven civilians were killed. In addition, more than eighty people were wounded, the majority of them civilians caught in the crossfire. However, although the civilian population of Limerick city would now be spared the sufferings of life in a battle zone, they had not seen the last of the conflict between the pro- and anti-Treaty forces.

On 28 August 1922, republican Captain Michael Danford was arrested in his cousin's house at 40 Roxboro Road in the city by three Free State army officers, who took Danford to the brickworks at Clino on the Tipperary road. Danford's bullet-ridden body was found there the following morning. A second Limerick republican, Harry Brazier, was killed by the Free State army at around the same time. Brazier was confronted by soldiers and shot dead while working in the locomotive yard at Limerick Station.

On 20 January 1923, two Clare republicans – IRA Commandant Con McMahon and IRA Volunteer Patrick Hennessy – were executed by Free State army firing squads in Limerick prison. These were the only two official executions to take place in Limerick – this is largely due to Donncadh O'Hannigan's opposition to the policy of executions whether official or secret. Not all Free State officers supported the policy of executions particularly when it involved men who had been active during the War of Independence. Michael Brennan, however, seemed to support the executions, since in addition to the two executions in Limerick prison, three republicans were executed in the divisional area under his command. All five were members of the IRA's Mid Clare Brigade and I feel it is necessary to ask whether they were singled out because of the intense and often bitter rivalry that had existed between Brennan's East Clare Brigade and the Mid Clare Brigade during the War of Independence?

O'Hannigan had the most successful fighting record of any flying column leader to join the Free State army. Both he and Brennan had come under suspicion for their negotiations with Lynch in July of 1922. Brennan managed to expunge any suspicion from his record by proving his loyalty to the Free State through his support of the executions and he eventually became head of the Irish army. However, a cloud of suspicion remained over O'Hannigan and while he was allowed to retain his rank, his military career did not prosper. After the Civil War O'Hannigan ended up as a 'Land Officer' for the Department of Defence.

Kerry IRA leader Tom McEllistrim later said: 'I knew the war was over when we left Limerick'.[84] With the capture of Waterford, Bruree and Cork in quick succession, by the Free

State army, the IRA was again forced to resort to guerrilla rather than conventional warfare. After 11 August, when Fermoy barracks fell to Free State troops, the republicans no longer held a single military installation. A Free State victory was now assured, but the Civil War had not yet reached its bloody pinnacle and would drag on for another nine months after the fall of Limerick. The Free State army eventually defeated the republicans. Approximately 1,500 people were killed during the Civil War, including 350 IRA volunteers, 730 Free State soldiers and 400 civilians. £47 million worth of damage had been done to the infrastructure of the country and the cost to the Irish people was even higher, as they were left bitterly divided for decades afterwards.

A few weeks after the fighting in Limerick city ended, IRA leader Frank Aiken, who was at that time trying to stay neutral, made an appeal for peace: 'War with the foreigner brings to the fore all that is best and noblest in a nation. Civil War all that is mean and base.'[85] Ultimately he was right. Aiken himself failed to remain neutral and threw in his lot with the republicans a short time later in late July 1922. He took over as IRA chief-of-staff after Lynch's death and issued the ceasefire order of 30 April 1923 which effectively ended the military conflict. The Civil War remains one of the saddest chapters in Irish history.

APPENDIX 1

CASUALTY LISTS FOR LIMERICK, 11–21 JULY 1922

Note: The following casualty lists have been compiled using period documents from the Irish Military Archives, newspaper accounts of the time and personal accounts from veterans of the fighting. However, these lists are not complete and may be subject to error. The *Limerick Chronicle* reported that Lieutenant Frank Teeling of the Free State army had been killed during the fighting in Limerick city, whereas in fact he had only been wounded and lived until 1976! It is very difficult in the fog of war to fix precisely the names and exact date of each casualty. The Civil War in Limerick was no exception, as the following account from *The Irish Times* of Wednesday 26 July, 1922, shows:

'Dead' Soldier Returns Home

The supposed remains of Private M. Bradley, who was reported killed at Limerick, were taken to Ballinasloe for internment. The parents on examining the remains were not satisfied as to their identity and had enquiries made at Galway, where he was last seen. In the meantime prayers were offered in the churches for the dead soldier, and the remains were interred by the Bradley family, a full military funeral being accorded. When the funeral was over and the people had returned from the burial ground, however, the real Private Bradley arrived home from Galway in a motor car to the great joy of his parents and relatives.

Republican Fatalities

Bh-Fian Michael Moynihan. From Sandmall Limerick. Died of wounds, 12 July 1922, Ordnance barracks Limerick city.

IRA Volunteer Patrick O'Mahony, Macroom, Cork. Killed in action Limerick city, 17 July 1922. Buried in Old Kilmurray cemetery, Co. Cork.

IRA Captain Paddy Naughton, Edward Street, Limerick. Killed in action Limerick city, 19 July 1922.

IRA Volunteer Slattery. Killed in action at Crossagalla, Co. Limerick in the retreat from the city.

Possibly also IRA Volunteer Seán Hogan. Killed in action 13 July 1922. Buried in the republican plot, Mount Saint Lawrence cemetery, Limerick.

Republican Casualties

Wounded – P. O'Connor stationed at Castle barracks Limerick.

Free State Fatalities

Private Thomas O'Brien, Upper William Street, Limerick city. Killed in action, Nelson Street, Limerick city, 11 July 1922.

Sergeant Patrick Stapleton 55751. Killed in action, Limerick city, 12 July 1922.

Private Joseph McEnery 8515, Clonroadmore, Ennis. Killed in action at Limerick city docks, 17 July 1922.

Private Peter Hanley VR11401. Killed in action, Limerick city, July 1922.

Private Tom Byrne. Killed in action.

Private Tweedy. Killed in action.

Free State Casualties

Captain Gerard Quinn, Corbally.

Colonel D. Ryan.

Colonel David Reynolds, Cork.

Private Francis Cassidy, Killaloe (?).

Captain James Hannon, Ardsollus, Dromoland, Co. Clare.

Captain Con O'Halloran, Ennis. Wounded in the right lung in the Strand barracks.

Lieutenant Frank Teeling, Dublin. Wounded during the attack on Munster Fair Tavern.

Civilian Fatalities

Bridie O'Brien, Bank Place, Limerick.

Mary Cadden, 1 New Road, Limerick.

Michael Kavanagh, Thomondgate, Limerick.

Patrick Hanley, Limerick (possibly Private Peter Hanley mentioned above).

Ellen Windrim, Dominick Street, Limerick.

John Noonan, Parnell Street, Limerick.

Edward Wallace, Watergate, Limerick.

Mr O'Mahony, O'Connell Street, Limerick.

Patrick O'Leary, Limerick.

Miss McKenna, Waterford.

Kennedy, Limerick.

O'Mahoney, Enniscorthy.

Appendix 2

Biographies

Michael Brennan (Free State army)

From Meelick in south-east Clare. Brennan had a well-earned reputation as a tenacious fighter and guerrilla leader. A member of the underground revolutionary conspiracy, the Irish Republican Brotherhood, since his teens, he had suffered imprisonment in Frongoch internment camp in Wales after the Easter Rising, and was a key figure in organising the Mountjoy hunger strike of 1917. During the War of Independence he was constantly on the run from British forces and had personally led several ambushes and barracks' raids, including the Glenwood ambush in East Clare, during which three Black and Tans and three members of the RIC were killed. On one occasion, when an RIC man had been alerted to the presence of Brennan's flying column and an RIC patrol refused to leave their barracks, Brennan stood alone in the street in front of the building and issued them a challenge to come out and fight. This was refused. Brennan also led a handful of men into O'Brien's Bridge, Limerick, in broad daylight and shot dead two RIC men. John Ryan, who was under Brennan's command that day, later commented: 'I believe that on the same day Brennan was in the mood that if this opportunity had not presented itself he would have gone right into the RIC barracks rather than leave the place without getting one of the enemy.'[86]

In 1921 Brennan had been promoted to divisional commander of the 1st Western Division by IRA headquarters. However, Brennan's War of Independence military career was marred by a bitter and intense personal feud between him and brothers Joe and Frank Barrett, the leaders of the neighbouring Mid Clare Brigade. After the signing of the Treaty it had been debatable as to which side Brennan would take in the conflict. John P. Duggan argues that ultimately the Barretts' support for the republican side was as important an influence on Brennan's decision to support the Free State, as his principles were.[87] Brennan later became leader of the Irish army and published his memoir of the period, *The War in Clare* (Four Courts Press, 1980).

Liam Lynch (IRA)

The commander of the IRA's 1st Southern Division. Though often claimed as a Cork man, he was actually from Angelsboro in Limerick. In 1914 he had joined Conradh na Gaeilge and might have confined his patriotism to cultural activities had he not been living in Fermoy and witnessed the dramatic events there in the immediate aftermath of the 1916 Rising.

On 1 May 1916, the RIC surrounded the house of the Kent family in Fermoy to arrest the family's sons. The Kent brothers resisted arrest and a prolonged firefight ensued. Richard was mortally wounded in the battle before the Kent family surrendered to the RIC. Thomas Kent was executed two days later by a British firing squad.

Liam Lynch had witnessed the fight from the town's bridge and that night swore that he would dedicate his life to the struggle for Irish freedom. He joined the Irish Volunteers in 1917 and became a member of the IRB some time later. In September 1919 he was wounded while leading an ambush to disarm a British army church parade at Fermoy. One British soldier – Private Jones – was killed in the struggle. However the operation was successful and Lynch's unit captured fifteen rifles. After being appointed commander of the IRA's 2nd North Cork Brigade, he kidnapped General Lucas of the British army, planning to use him to exchange for IRA prisoners under sentence of death.

Lynch was arrested in August 1920, but was released after undertaking a brief hunger strike. Lynch's most successful military operation was the raid on the British military barracks in Mallow in September 1920. Led by himself and Ernie O'Malley, the IRA captured two Hotchkiss machine-guns, twenty-seven rifles, one revolver and 4,000 rounds of ammunition.

Lynch's record as a guerrilla leader and his determination to secure the Irish republic against all enemies made him a formidable opponent for Michael Brennan and the other Free State army officers in Limerick. Lynch was a dogmatic republican and was not prepared to compromise on the issue of complete Irish independence, and had stated this bluntly in a letter to his brother after he joined the Irish Volunteers in 1917. 'We have declared for an Irish Republic and will not live under any other law.'[88] Having committed to the republican struggle Lynch was prepared to see it through to a bitter and bloody end – even if that meant fighting his former comrades in Limerick city. Lynch was shot dead by Free State army troops in the Knockmealdown Mountains on 10 April 1923 and was succeeded as IRA chief-of-staff by Frank Aiken.

William Murphy (Free State army)

Born in Wexford in 1890. He had been orphaned at an early age and raised by his cousins in Belfast where he settled and found work as a schoolteacher on the Falls Road. In 1915 Murphy joined the South Staffordshire Regiment of the British army. During the First World War he fought in the battles of the Somme, High Wood and Deville Wood. In 1917 he was promoted to captain and awarded the Military Cross. In 1919 he retired from the British army with the rank of lieutenant colonel. He returned to Ireland and was appointed inspector of schools in Derry. When the Provisional Government founded the Free State army, Murphy was head-hunted by Michael Collins and given a commission in the new force on the merit of his career in the British army.

Eoin O'Duffy (Free State army)

O'Duffy was born near Castleblaney, County Monaghan, in 1890. He was a leading member of the GAA and active in Conradh na Gaeilge, but did not join the IRA until 1917. He had been imprisoned in Belfast jail and led a hunger strike by republican prisoners there. He had initially earned a reputation for himself in republican circles for capturing and destroying Ballytrain RIC barracks in February of 1920. However, his subsequent fighting record in the IRA was far less spectacular, comprising mainly executions of suspected British spies, a few on somewhat dubious grounds. During the War of Independence O'Duffy had lost the index finger on his left hand. He later made the claim that it had been shot off in a gun battle with the Black and Tans, when in fact he had accidentally shot himself with an automatic pistol.

O'Duffy was appointed garda commissioner in 1922 and held the post until 1932. He became leader of the Irish Fascist movement 'The Blueshirts' and helped found the Fine Gael Party in 1933. During the Second World War, he disseminated pro-Nazi and anti-semitic propaganda in Ireland. His political career ended in failure, and he became an alcoholic, dying in a nursing home in 1944.

T. O'Gorman (IRA)

An enigmatic figure. O'Gorman had been appointed divisional adjutant of the 2nd Western Division by IRA headquarters in Dublin. It seems that local IRA leaders in the area found his presence somewhat of an inconvenience. According to Tom Maguire:

> O'Gorman an ... [unclear] in the British army once. He had been a deserter from the British army and had been around the south with the IRA, he had been appointed by GHQ, later when I talked to Liam Lynch about him he was amazed that he had been appointed Divisional Adjutant. He was a devil for drink and would then come to me craving for forgiveness.[89]

Ernie O'Malley (IRA)

O'Malley was born in Castlebar, County Mayo, in 1897. When O'Malley was a teenager his parents moved to Dublin. O'Malley was studying medicine at University College Dublin in 1916 when the Rising broke out. Though he had no prior involvement in politics, or connections with the rebels, acting on impulse O'Malley and a friend managed to get hold of a rifle and fire a few shots at British troops during the fighting. O'Malley formally joined the IRA in 1918 and was eventually appointed as a training officer for rural IRA units. In February 1920, he led the IRA attack on an RIC barracks in Ballytrain, County Monaghan, with Eoin O'Duffy. In September 1920 he and Liam Lynch led the attack and capture of the British army barracks in Mallow, County Cork. He was arrested in possession of a handgun in Kilkenny in December 1920 and was facing execution when he escaped from Kilmainham jail on 21 February 1921.

In 1922 O'Malley was part of the force that occupied the

Four Courts garrison. He escaped from Free State custody after the surrender of the Four Courts at the beginning of the Civil War and travelled to Wicklow and Wexford to rally the local IRA units. He returned to Dublin whilst 'on the run' and was captured again and seriously wounded after a shoot-out with Free State troops in the Ballsbridge in November 1922. O'Malley spent the rest of the Civil War in prison and was one of the last republican prisoners to be released following the end of hostilities. His two books *On Another Man's Wound* (Anvil, revised edition 2002) and *The Singing Flame* (Anvil, 1992) are widely regarded as two of the best accounts of the period.

ENDNOTES

1   Captured Documents Collection. Irish Military Archives 177/1/A.

2   Sheehan, William, *British Voices From The Irish War of Independence 1918–1921* (The Collins Press, 2005) pp. 149–150.

3   Robert Barton, Bureau of Military History Witness Statement No. 979, p. 44.

4   Ó Fathaigh, Pádraig, *Memoirs of a Galway Gaelic Leaguer* (Irish Lives Series, Cork University Press, 2000) p. 86.

5   *Limerick Leader*, 20 February 1922.

6   Hartnet, Mossie, *Victory and Woe* (UCD Press, 2002) p. 123.

7   Hopkinson, Michael, *Green Against Green: The Irish Civil War* (Gill and Macmillan, 1988) p. 64.

8   Anon., 'The 43rd in Ireland', *Oxfordshire and Buckinghamshire Light Infantry Regimental Chronicle*, p. 149.

9   O'Malley, Ernie, *The Singing Flame* (Anvil Press, 1992) p. 61.

10 *Ibid.*, pp. 56–57.

11 *Ibid.*, pp. 57–58.

12 *Ibid.*, pp. 59–60.

13 Hopkinson, Michael, *Green Against Green: The Irish Civil War* (Gill and Macmillan, 1988) p. 63.

14   McEoin, Uinseann, *Survivors* (Argenta Publications, 1980) p. 230.

15   *Limerick Leader*, 10 March 1922.

16   Valiulis, Maryann Gialanella, *Richard Mulcahy and the founding of the Irish Free State* (Irish Academic Press, 1992) p. 132.

17   Hopkinson, Michael, *Green Against Green: The Irish Civil War* (Gill and Macmillan, 1988) p. 63.

18   Oscar Traynor, O'Malley Papers P17B/95, UCD Archives.

19   Younger, Calton, *Ireland's Civil War* (Fontana Books, 1970) p. 244.

20   Hopkinson, Michael, *Green Against Green: The Irish Civil War* (Gill and Macmillan, 1988) p. 64.

21   Coogan, Tim Pat & Morrison, George, *The Irish Civil War* (Orion Publishing, 1999) p. 141.

22   Hopkinson, Michael, *Green Against Green: The Irish Civil War* (Gill and Macmillan, 1988) p. 65.

23   *Limerick Chronicle*, 6 April 1922.

24   Pinkman, John, *In the Legion of the Vanguard* (edited by Francis E. Maguire, Mercier Press, 1998) pp. 85–86.

25   *Ibid.*, pp. 171–174.

26   Ryan, P.J., 'The Fourth Siege Of Limerick: Civil War July 1922', *The Old Limerick Journal*, Winter 2002, p. 10.

27   O'Malley, Ernie, *The Singing Flame* (Anvil Press, 1992) pp. 84–85.

28   Hopkinson, Michael, *Green Against Green: The Irish Civil War* (Gill and Macmillan, 1988) p. 115.

29   Ó Snodaigh, Aengus, 'The RAF and Ireland 1922–1926', *Irish Sword* Vol XVII No. 68, pp. 183–185.

30   Walsh, P.V., 'The Irish Civil War, 1922-23', *New York Military Affairs Symposium*, 1998, p. 9.

31 O'Malley, Ernie, *The Singing Flame* (Anvil Press, 1992) p. 97.

32 From the Regimental Chronicle quoted in Stanley C. Jenkins, 'The Oxfordshire and Buckinghamshire Light Infantry in Ireland 1919-23', *Soldiers of Oxfordshire Trust 'Sword and Bugle'*, 2009.

33 For more see Ryan, Meda, *The Real Chief: Liam Lynch* (Mercier Press, 2005) pp. 139–142.

34 Litton, Helen, *The Irish Civil War: An Illustrated History*, (Wolfhound Press, 2001) p. 72.

35 McMahon, Paul, *British Spies & Irish Rebels. British Intelligence and Ireland 1916–1945* (The Boydell Press, 2008) p. 85.

36 Younger, Calton, *Ireland's Civil War* (Fontana Books, 1970) p. 371.

37 *Ibid.*, p. 370.

38 *Ibid.*, p. 372–5.

39 Irish Military Archives 177/1/A.

40 *Ibid.*

41 Younger, Calton, *Ireland's Civil War* (Fontana Books, 1970) p. 378.

42 Hopkinson, Michael, *Green Against Green: The Irish Civil War* (Gill and Macmillan, 1988) p. 146.

43 *Cork Examiner*, 17 July 1922.

44 Hopkinson, Michael, *Green Against Green: The Irish Civil War* (Gill and Macmillan, 1988) p. 147.

45 *Ibid.*, p. 147.

46 Captured Papers Collection. Irish Military Archives; Ryan, Meda, *The Real Chief: Liam Lynch* (Mercier, 2005) pp. 146–147.

47 Younger, Calton, *Ireland's Civil War* (Fontana Books, 1970) p. 375.

48   Hopkinson, Michael, *Green Against Green: The Irish Civil War* (Gill and Macmillan, 1988) p. 148

49   A/0991/2 in Lot 3 Captured Papers Collection, Irish Military Archives.

50   *Ibid.*, p. 149.

51   Michael Lawless, Bureau of Military History Witness Statement 727, pp. 5–6.

52   Lot 3 Captured Papers Collection. Irish Military Archives; Hopkinson, Michael, *Green Against Green: The Irish Civil War* (Gill and Macmillan 1988) p. 149.

53   Hopkinson, Michael, *Green Against Green: The Irish Civil War* (Gill and Macmillan, 1988) p. 149.

54   McEoin, Uinseann, *Survivors* (Argenta Publications, 1980) pp. 245–246.

55   McMahon, Tony, 'Studiisque Asperrima Belli', *The Old Limerick Journal*, Volume 8, Autumn 1981, pp. 30–31.

56   Deasy, Liam, *Brother Against Brother* (Mercier Press Cork, 1998) pp. 58–59.

57   Joe Graham interview with Tom Toomey, August 1989. Later on in the Civil War Hayes, Graham and O'Brien found themselves as prisoners in Cork under Dan Breen's command. Breen feared that they would be shot in reprisal after the Free State capture of Cork in August 1922, and so he took them to the main Cork–Dublin railway line, issued them with an IRA pass to guarantee their safety and told them to start walking for Dublin and not look back. Dan Breen is still seen by some as 'a thug with blood on his hands' (Ambrose, Joe, *Dan Breen and the IRA* (Mercier Press, 2007) p. 8) but the efforts he made to try and stop the slide into Civil War in 1922 and his part in saving the lives of these three men, has never been fully recognised.

58   *Clare Champion*, Saturday 15 July 1922.

59   Information received from Des Long, Joe Nash's son-in-law.

60   Irish Military Archives A/0944/2.

61   Pinkman, John A., *In the Legion of the Vanguard* (edited by Francis E. Maguire, Mercier Press, 1998) pp. 147–152.

62   McMahon, Tony, 'Studiisque Asperrima Belli', *The Old Limerick Journal*, Volume 8, Autumn 1981, p. 31.

63   Information from Pat Gunn, son of George Gunn.

64   *Clare Champion*, 29 July 1922.

65   *The Irish Times*, 21 July 1922.

66   'Padjoe' a derogative term used by Free State Soldiers to describe members of the IRA. See Pinkman, John A., *In the Legion of the Vanguard* (edited by Francis E. Maguire, Mercier Press, 1998) p. 97. 'We knew them as 'Irregulars' but when we saw for ourselves their inept tactics as soldiers and their dishonourable behaviour as Irishmen we contemptuously called them "Paddy Joes", or more colloquially "Padjoes" – a derogatory term equivalent to the English epitaph "yokels" or "bumpkins".'

67   Pinkman, John A., *In the Legion of the Vanguard* (edited by Francis E. Maguire, Mercier Press, 1998) pp. 147–152

68   McEoin, Uinseann, *Survivors* (Argenta Publications, 1980) p. 245.

69   Captured Documents Collection, Lot 3, Irish Military Archives. The fire engine never arrived in Limerick.

70   *The Republican Bulletin*, 19 July 1922.

71   The *Limerick Leader*, quoted in Corbett, Jim, *Not While I have Ammo. A history of Connie Mackey, Defender of the Strand* (Nonsuch Publications, 2008) p. 93.

72   *The Irish Times*, Saturday 22 July 1922.

73 Deasy, Liam, *Brother Against Brother* (Mercier Press, 1998) p. 65.

74 McEoin, Uinseann, *Survivors* (Argenta Publications, 1980) pp. 245–246.

75 Madge Daly, Bureau of Military History Witness Statement 855, p. 11.

76 McEoin, Uinseann, *Survivors* (Argenta Publications, 1980).

77 McMahon, Tony, 'Studiisque Asperrima Belli', *The Old Limerick Journal*, Volume 8, Autumn 1981, p. 31.

78 *Clare Champion*, Saturday 29 July 1922.

79 Pinkman, John A., *In the Legion of the Vanguard*, (edited by Francis E. Maguire, Mercier Press, 1998) pp. 147–152.

80 McMahon, Tony, 'Studiisque Asperrima Belli', *The Old Limerick Journal*, Volume 8, Autumn 1981, p. 31.

81 *The Irish Times*, 21 July 1922.

82 Eoin O'Duffy to Michael Collins, 21 July 1922, UCD Archives P7/B/68.

83 UCD Archives, Mulcahy Papers, P7/B/40.

84 Dwyer, T. Ryle, *Tans, Terrors and Troubles* (Mercier Press, 2001) p. 354.

85 Frank Aiken in a letter to the Provisional (Free State) Government, 3 August 1922, Captured Documents Collection, Irish Military Archives 177/1/A.

86 John Ryan, Bureau of Military Witness Statement.

87 Duggan, John P., *A History of the Irish Army* (Gill and Macmillan, 1991) p. 78.

88 Ryan, Meda, *The Real Chief: Liam Lynch* (Mercier, 2005) p. 24.

89 O'Malley notebooks, UCD Archives, P17b/100.

INDEX